Cognitive Behavioral Therapy for Anxiety and Depression During Pregnancy and Beyond

This book is a hands-on guide for facilitating treatment of anxiety and depression during pregnancy and the postpartum period. Readers will learn about why anxiety and related difficulties can increase during pregnancy and the postpartum period, the critical roles that thoughts and behaviors play in maintaining symptoms, and how to apply practical cognitive and behavioral strategies to reduce distress and increase coping skills. Chapters are integrated with the latest research, and clinicians and individuals alike are presented with customizable cognitive behavioral therapy-based handouts, exercises, and worksheets proven to meet the unique needs of the perinatal population.

Sheryl M. Green, PhD, CPsych, is an assistant professor in the Department of Psychiatry and Behavioural Neurosciences at McMaster University and a clinical health psychologist in the Women's Health Concerns Clinic and Consultation Liaison Services at St. Joseph's Healthcare Hamilton in Ontario, Canada.

Benicio N. Frey, MD, PhD, is an associate professor in the Department of Psychiatry and Behavioural Neurosciences at McMaster University, medical director of the Women's Health Concerns Clinic, and academic head of the Mood Disorders Program at St. Joseph's Healthcare Hamilton.

Eleanor Donegan, PhD, is a clinical health psychologist and research analyst at the Women's Health Concerns Clinic at St. Joseph's Healthcare Hamilton.

Randi E. McCabe, PhD, CPsych, is a professor in the Department of Psychiatry and Behavioural Neurosciences at McMaster University. She is psychologist in chief and director of the Anxiety Treatment and Research Clinic at St. Joseph's Healthcare Hamilton.

Cognitive Behavioral Therapy for Anxiety and Depression During Pregnancy and Beyond

How to Manage Symptoms and Maximize Well-Being

Sheryl M. Green, Benicio N. Frey, Eleanor Donegan, and Randi E. McCabe

Routledge
Taylor & Francis Group

NEW YORK AND LONDON

First published 2019
by Routledge
52 Vanderbilt Ave, New York, NY 10017

and by Routledge
2 Park Square, Milton Park, Abingdon, Oxon, OX14 4RN

Routledge is an imprint of the Taylor & Francis Group, an informa business

Library of Congress Cataloging-in-Publication Data
Names: Green, Sheryl M., author.
Title: Cognitive behavioral therapy for anxiety and depression during pregnancy and beyond : how to manage symptoms and maximize well-being / Sheryl M. Green, Benicio N. Frey, Eleanor Donegan, and Randi E. McCabe.
Description: New York : Routledge, 2019. | Includes bibliographical references and index.
Identifiers: LCCN 2018032506| ISBN 9781138201095 (hardcover : alk. paper) | ISBN 9781138201118 (pbk. : alk. paper) | ISBN 9781315452494 (e-book)
Subjects: LCSH: Depression, Mental–Treatment. | Pregnancy–Psychological aspects. | Women–Health and hygiene.
Classification: LCC RC537 .G7214 2019 | DDC 616.85/27–dc23
LC record available at https://lccn.loc.gov/2018032506

ISBN: 978-1-138-20109-5 (hbk)
ISBN: 978-1-138-20111-8 (pbk)
ISBN: 978-1-315-45249-4 (ebk)

Typeset in Garamond
by Swales & Willis Ltd, Exeter, Devon, UK

For my beautiful daughters, Claire and Ana, and for Elaine,
my loving mother
S. M. G.

To my beloved wife, Daniela, and my two treasures, Bruno and Leo
B. N. F.

To my family, Julie, Gerald, and Chris, for always providing love and
encouragement. I am very grateful for your support

E. D.

For my mother, Gail McCabe, who has always been unwavering in love
and support

R. E. M.

Contents

PART III
Other Approaches to Enhance Well-Being: Medication and Support..... 173

Figures, Tables, and Forms

Figures

Tables

Forms

Acknowledgments

We would like to thank the women we work with, day to day, at the Women's Health Concerns Clinic and particularly those who participated in the cognitive behavioral therapy group for perinatal anxiety. By allowing us to engage in their care and trusting us with their shared experiences, they have helped to educate us on the uniqueness of anxiety during pregnancy and the postpartum period.

We would also like to thank the leadership of the of mental health and addictions program at St. Joseph's Healthcare Hamilton, including Dr. Peter Bieling and Ms. Sharon Simons, for fostering a culture of inquiry and providing support for research. We are also grateful to The Research Institute of St. Joseph's Healthcare and the Teresa Cascioli Charitable Foundation. Their support enabled us to continue the development of this research program and provide an important treatment option for women experiencing anxiety during pregnancy and the postpartum period.

Warm appreciation to Anna, our very patient editor, and the other members of the editing and publishing team at Routledge.

Finally, deep gratitude to our spouses and family members for their continuing support and understanding during the writing of this book.

Introduction

I worried about getting pregnant again following my miscarriage and now that I am pregnant, my anxiety has increased. Lately my worry revolves around whether there is or will be something wrong with my baby and how I will handle labor and delivery.

(Cassandra, 31 years old, 4 months pregnant)

I remember how much work there was when my first son arrived. Caring for a newborn was all consuming and I felt like I barely got by. Now that my second baby will be arriving shortly, I fear that I will not be able to handle two children. I also worry that the relationship I built with my son will end as I will have no quality time with him.

(Juanita, 43 years old, 8 months pregnant)

As soon as I became a mother I was very anxious about caring for my baby properly and being a good parent. I check on my daughter multiple times in the night and watch her sleep, fearing that she will stop breathing. My sister, mother, and mother-in-law are all great mothers and I find myself asking for their advice in caring for my daughter many times throughout the day even when I know the answer.

(Zoë, 23 years old, 4 weeks postpartum)

Anxiety was never a problem for me in the past, so when I started worrying about what others thought of me and my parenting or doing the 'right' thing, with bottle feeding for example, it was so upsetting that I started going out less and doubting myself more.

(Keesha, 29 years old, 3 months postpartum)

Prior to going on maternity leave, my career had been such a big part of my life and something I enjoyed. I worry that when

1

I return to work I will not be able to balance family life, my relationship with my husband, and my career. I fear so much that I will make the wrong decisions that I have felt more depressed.

(Elizabeth, 38 years old, 7 months postpartum)

Every woman's experience of pregnancy and the time directly following pregnancy (the postpartum period) is unique. Although having a baby is a natural biological process (resulting in 372,000 births a day worldwide!) pregnancy and the postpartum period may be accompanied by a number of physical and emotional experiences that can significantly impact a woman, both positively and negatively. Unfortunately, these negative emotional experiences may escalate to the point that symptoms of anxiety and depression may greatly affect day-to-day well-being and functioning. Most people are familiar with the term 'postpartum depression.' Postpartum depression is more than just the 'baby blues.' It refers to the development of a serious episode of mood symptoms that begins in the days or weeks following the birth of a baby. These symptoms can last from weeks to months and often worsen without treatment. Mothers with postpartum depression may find it increasingly difficult to take care of themselves, let alone their baby or the things that they need to do throughout the day. Research shows that for many women with postpartum depression the mood symptoms actually began during pregnancy.

Recent studies have revealed that *anxiety* is more common than depression during pregnancy and just as common, if not more so, during the postpartum period (e.g., Giardinelli et al., 2012). Anxiety during this time can take away the enjoyment of pregnancy and the transition to motherhood. Anxiety often leads to self-doubt and loss of confidence, withdrawal from family and friends, and avoidance of activities one previously enjoyed. Anxiety can take many forms — from daily worry and apprehension that make life seem like a struggle to incapacitating and intense episodes of physical symptoms called panic attacks that make you feel like there is something really wrong with you or an intense feeling that you might die.

You may have struggled with anxiety or depression at different times in your life and find that, since becoming pregnant or having your baby, the symptoms are starting to intensify. On the other hand, you may never have had difficulties with anxiety or depression prior to your pregnancy and now discover yourself having to deal with these symptoms for the first time. Either way, you are not alone. Research shows that one in five women experience significant difficulties with anxiety or depression during pregnancy and the postpartum period (Falah-Hassani et al., 2017).

How This Book Can Help

This book is intended for any woman who may be pregnant or a new mother who is having difficulties managing symptoms of anxiety and depression. Whether you are on your first pregnancy or your fifth, we designed this book to effectively help you manage your anxiety and depressive symptoms using effective psychological and behavioral techniques based on scientific evidence. The treatment approach offered in this book addresses a real gap that we saw in current available treatment options. Many of the pregnant women and new mothers who are referred to our clinic experience anxiety as a primary problem, yet available treatments, such as medication in the form of anti-anxiety agents or anti-depressants, are often not preferred or simply not recommended by their prescribing physician. Moreover, when women do take medications they often report that the relief they experience from symptoms of anxiety and depression is not enough. Like these women, you may be in one of the groups shown in Figure 0.1.

Cognitive Behavioral Therapy

Cognitive behavioral therapy or CBT is a psychological and behavioral treatment approach that is highly effective for addressing the symptoms of anxiety and depression, as well as a range of health issues, including chronic pain. In fact, over the past few decades, CBT has become a *first-line* psychological treatment for anxiety disorders because of the numerous research studies demonstrating how effective it is (Otte, 2011). CBT focuses on understanding how your thoughts, behaviors, physical symptoms, and your environment interact to cause you distress. Using CBT, you will learn a number of specific strategies to reduce unhelpful thought patterns and to improve your behavioral responses to uncomfortable symptoms and stressors.

How This Program Works

This book is designed to help you manage symptoms of anxiety and depression during pregnancy and after you have had your baby. Part I will help you learn more

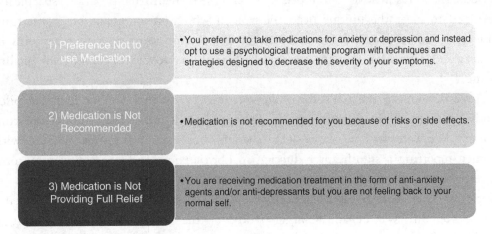

Figure 0.1 Considerations with Medication

about anxiety and depression in general and understand why so many women tend to develop symptoms during pregnancy and after delivery. Part I also explains the cognitive behavioral treatment approach in detail, including what it is, how it works, and what is required of you so that you know what to expect and what you can do to maximize the benefits you receive from this program. Part II includes the *treatment chapters*, which provide specific cognitive and behavioral strategies tailored to the unique needs of women during pregnancy and the transition to motherhood. The content in these chapters will allow you to target your symptoms directly to reduce distress and enhance your well-being. Part III provides information on medication approaches, which may be indicated for women who have more severe symptoms or for those whose symptoms do not fully improve with psychotherapy. Part III also provides information on how to make the most of your support network as well as information for your family and friends on how to best provide you with support. We know from research that activating a woman's support system is a major factor in helping her to overcome symptoms and enhance her well-being so that she is in a better position to care for herself and her baby.

How This Book Came About

At St. Joseph's Healthcare in Hamilton, Ontario, we work in a specialty clinic that provides services to women suffering from mood and anxiety disorders across the reproductive milestones (e.g., pregnancy, postpartum, menopause). The Women's Health Concerns Clinic receives referrals for women who have depression following the birth of their baby, also known as postpartum depression. Although postpartum depression affects a substantial number of women (about 9–19%: O'Hara & Wisner, 2014), in recent years we have recognized that even more referrals were being sent on behalf of pregnant and postpartum women suffering from *anxiety* as their primary problem. Despite the fact that CBT is the first-line psychological treatment for anxiety disorders, no formal treatment manuals were available for the perinatal period. As a result, we developed a CBT-based treatment program specifically designed to meet the unique needs of women who were pregnant or postpartum. This program is designed for pregnant or postpartum women with symptoms of anxiety and depression that interfere with their ability to function and their quality of life.

After developing the CBT for anxiety treatment manual we conducted a pilot study to evaluate the effectiveness of this program for pregnant and postpartum women. We were very pleased to learn that the treatment was a great success, with women reporting a significant reduction in both anxiety and depression symptoms (Green et al., 2015). Importantly, the treatment was also very well received by participants, as women reported high levels of satisfaction following the perinatal CBT program. We began a larger study of the treatment program using a randomized controlled trial design where we compared the symptoms of women participating in the CBT program to women on a waiting list for treatment. In the final phase of this study, we are finding robust reductions in symptoms of anxiety and depression for women participating in this new perinatal CBT program compared to those on the waiting list who are not receiving treatment.

Given our research findings, we wanted to make this treatment program more accessible to women outside our community. We also wanted to provide the treatment in the form of a workbook so that it could be used by pregnant women and new mothers either on their own or with the aid of their healthcare provider (psychologist, social worker, mental health clinician). Although there are a number of workbooks available for anxiety, we found that there was a strong need for a book with an approach tailored to the specific needs of women during pregnancy and the transition to motherhood.

References

Falah-Hassani, K., Shiri, R., & Dennis, C. L. (2017). The prevalence of antenatal and postnatal co-morbid anxiety and depression: A meta-analysis. *Psychological Medicine, 47*, 2041–2053.

Giardinelli, L., Innocenti, A., Benni, L., Stefanini, M. C., Lino, G., Lunardi, C., ... Faravelli, C. (2012). Depression and anxiety in the perinatal period: Prevalence and risk factors in an Italian sample. *Archives of Women's Mental Health, 15*, 21–30. doi:10.1007/s00737-011-0249-8

Green, S. M., Haber, E., Frey, B. N., & McCabe, R. E. (2015). Cognitive-behavioral group treatment for perinatal anxiety: A pilot study. *Archives of Women's Mental Health, 18*, 631–638. doi:10.1007/s00737-015-0498-z

O'Hara, M. W., & Wisner, K. L. (2014). Perinatal mental illness: Definition, description and aetiology. *Best Practice and Research: Clinical Obstetrics and Gynaecology, 28*, 3–12.

Otte, C. (2011). Cognitive behavioral therapy in anxiety disorders: Current state of the evidence. *Dialogues in Clinical Neuroscience, 13*, 413–421.

Part I

Anxiety and Depression During Pregnancy and Beyond

Understanding Symptoms and the CBT Approach

Chapter 1

Understanding Anxiety During Pregnancy and the Postpartum Period

A Vulnerable Time

What is Anxiety?

Why am I Having an Increase in Anxiety During Pregnancy and the Postpartum?

When Should I Seek Treatment for my Anxiety?

People who have difficulties with anxiety are often surprised to learn that it is a *normal*, natural, emotional, and physical reaction that all people experience – often on a daily basis. You might be even more surprised to learn that it serves an important role in our daily lives by alerting us to danger and generating a fear response that can save our lives in day-to-day occurrences. For instance, consider the following scenarios. You decide to cross the street after determining that the coast is clear. You begin to proceed but notice in the corner of your eye a car darting out on to the road headed straight for your path. At that point, you do not have time to think 'wow, that car is really going fast, I should probably get out of the way' – you just do it! That is an example of anxiety and the fear response saving your life! Or perhaps you have an interview scheduled for your dream job the following day. Do you stay up late or possibly try to get a good night's sleep by going to bed at a reasonable time? Do you say you will 'wing it' or perhaps spend some time preparing with responses to anticipated questions? Do you show up in your pajamas or do you choose your outfit the night before? Anxiety plays a role in all of these circumstances and decisions by alerting you to the possibility of danger and motivating you to prepare to cope with a high-stakes situation. In many situations, the danger isn't a physical one as it is in the scenario of being hit by a car, it is in the form of a performance situation where you could lose out if you do not do well, such as reducing your chances of getting the dream job that you have an interview for.

When we are anxious, it is not just an emotional experience – there are physical and thought components as well. Physically, we feel it in our bodies with common symptoms such as a racing heart, hotness or sweating, chest pain or pressure, shortness of breath, dizziness or lightheadedness, and tingling or numbness in your arms and legs to name a few. These physical symptoms can be very uncomfortable, or even scary, to experience. So why does this happen? Read on to get some insight into our amazing physiology and understand how our nervous system works.

The Physical Component of Anxiety (Our 'Fight or Flight' System)

The autonomic nervous system, more commonly known as our *'fight or flight'* system, is a part of the nervous system that controls and regulates our internal organs. Interestingly, this does not require any effort on our part and in fact, we are not even aware that this is happening – our body just does it automatically! The autonomic nervous system is made up of two subsystems: (1) the *sympathetic nervous system* and (2) the *parasympathetic nervous system*. These two systems work closely together to control our energy levels and to help our bodies prepare for action when we are in danger.

How Does It Work?

When we perceive danger (or even when we simply anticipate danger) our brain starts by activating the *sympathetic nervous system*. When this system is activated, there is a release of hormones (e.g., epinephrine (adrenaline) and norepinephrine (noradrenaline)) that brings about changes in the body very quickly to help us prepare to *fight or flee*. These changes may affect cardiovascular function (e.g., increased heart rate, changes in blood flow), respiration (e.g., increased rate of breathing), and temperature regulation (e.g., increased sweating). Importantly, the sympathetic nervous system operates on an 'all-or-none' principle. That is, once it is activated, all or most of the systems that could help you *fight* the danger that you are faced with or *flee*/run away from the danger become activated regardless of the situation. This explains why we often experience more than one physical symptom when we are anxious. For further reading about the fight-or-flight response, Barlow and Craske (2007) provide a summary. Have a look at Figure 1.1 to understand some of the other bodily changes that take place and the functions they serve when the sympathetic nervous system is activated during a *fight or flight* response.

Although the bodily sensations associated with our *fight or flight* response can be very uncomfortable (and they should be – otherwise we wouldn't act to protect ourselves!) we want to emphasize here that these symptoms are *not* dangerous and are part of the body's powerful and adaptive system to protect you from harm. It is also very important to note that these changes are *transient*. Over time, the

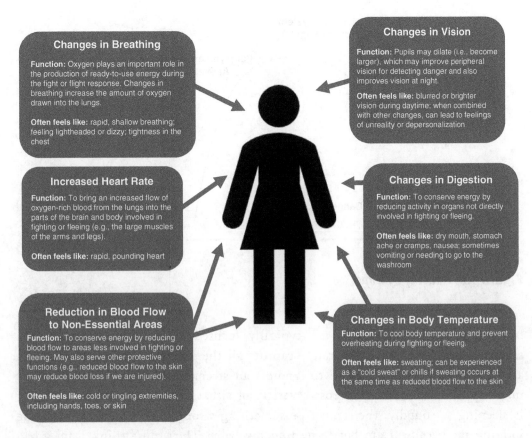

Figure 1.1   Impact of Autonomic Nervous System

parasympathetic nervous system is activated. This system is also automatic and reverses the bodily changes produced by the sympathetic nervous system (e.g., returning breathing rate to normal, slowing heart rate, re-starting digestion). This is important because many of the people we treat for anxiety difficulties express concerns that their anxiety will simply continue to increase forever or will increase to harmful levels. In fact, with the parasympathetic nervous system, we have a built-in recovery system that is specifically designed to calm us down over time. However, this system tends to be cautious and it may take longer for symptoms associated with anxiety to decrease than it took for the sympathetic nervous system to produce them (Figure 1.2).

The Thought Component of Anxiety

The thought component of anxiety is often experienced in the form of worry. Worries tend to focus on the future and the bad things that might happen or be out of your control. Based on our two examples above, worries might sound something like, 'What if I say something stupid or wrong during the job interview tomorrow' or 'This is a dangerous intersection, I am going to get hit

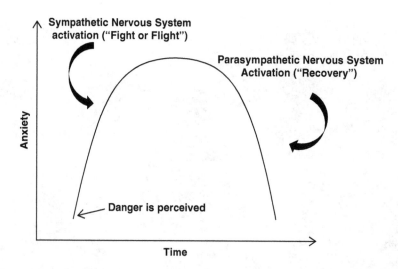

Figure 1.2 Anxiety by Time

by a car.' Anxious thoughts are typically focused on danger or threat in a situation and tend not to accurately capture all the information in a situation in a balanced way. They also tend to ignore your strengths or ability to cope. They may happen automatically, across a variety of situations. For example, 'My baby is sleeping so soundly, there must be something wrong with him' or 'People are judging me because I am bottle feeding my baby. They must think I am a bad mother.'

There are definitely times in life when anxiety very naturally tends to increase. For instance, certain life transitions such as moving out on your own, starting a new school program or job, or life situations such as preparing for an exam, or dealing with ongoing conflict with a neighbor or boss, can all increase anxiety. Anxiety can be adaptive in these types of situations if we are able to respond in a functional way (e.g., by arranging a moving truck for the move, completing all the administrative paperwork before arriving on the first day of school, preparing in advance for the exam). As you can see through these examples, anxiety is actually helping us by motivating us to prepare and act. Although we can all agree that anxiety does not feel very comfortable when we experience it, it plays a crucial role in our daily lives.

However, problems with anxiety may emerge when you experience (1) *too much* anxiety and (2) anxiety at the *wrong time.* When you experience too much anxiety, even at appropriate times, it can be interfering and distressing in your life. In these times, your anxiety may exceed your ability to cope and manage in an effective way. It is also at this time that *anxiety is no longer helpful.* When anxiety comes about at the *wrong time* or at a time when you believe there is danger when there really is none (e.g., believing you missed a spot when you washed the baby bottles after having washed them twice already), it is not helpful and in fact can reduce your ability to function on a daily basis and/or affect your quality of life.

Why Am I Experiencing so Much Anxiety during Pregnancy or the Postpartum Period?

A Biological Perspective

During pregnancy and the postpartum period women experience greater variation in their hormonal levels than in any other period of life. To put this into perspective, there are no medications or treatments that can increase the levels of hormones (e.g., estrogen and progesterone) to the same extent that a woman experiences *naturally* during her third trimester of pregnancy! Moreover, shortly after the baby is born a woman's hormone levels decrease almost 1,000-fold. Researchers believe that this extreme fluctuation of hormone levels likely increases the biological risks for anxiety and depression symptoms during pregnancy and the postpartum period, in addition to each woman's unique personal risk associated with her genetic makeup (Steiner et al., 2003). Other risk factors exist and will be discussed in the next section. For more information on the biological contributions to anxiety and depression symptoms, please see Chapter 11.

In Addition to the Biological Perspective ...

In addition to the biological factors that can increase anxiety during pregnancy and the postpartum period, a number of other factors can also contribute to anxiety during this time. Read the vignette below and engage in the following exercise to understand why pregnancy and the postpartum period can increase a woman's vulnerability to experience higher levels of anxiety, in addition to the biological changes that occur.

Meet Dahlia

Dahlia is a physically and mentally healthy 28-year-old woman who lives in Toronto with her husband of three years. She works as a high school teacher. Both her parents and in-laws live and work about an hour away, in the suburbs. She recently moved into a two-bedroom starter home, one bedroom of which is used as a storage room. She has a few close friends from high school whom she regularly sees to go shopping or out for dinner. Although some of her friends are also married, none have children. Dahlia is very active, playing soccer or running once a week. Further, she and her husband enjoy planning a bi-weekly 'date night' and drive to visit their families on long weekends.

Dahlia is now three months pregnant. Complete Form 1.1 to record what you think about her sitatuion.

Share Your Thoughts

What areas of Dahlia's life could be affected by both her pregnancy and the eventual addition of a child to her family? In what ways?

1. Hard to relate to friends and see them as much

2. Wont be much time for husband

3. Must make storage room into Baby Room

4. Parents too far away to be there when husband isnt

5. Probably wont be able to be as active as before

Form 1.1   Share Your Thoughts

The fact is, almost every area of life is impacted during pregnancy and when a woman becomes a new mother. Figure 1.3 shows a summary of a few of the major life areas that will be affected. See if the responses you gave are the same.

Here is a more detailed look at each area listed in Figure 1.3.

Physical and Body

One of the most obvious changes that a woman experiences when she becomes pregnant is her physical transformation. The body is working overtime to grow another human being and with this, two obvious physical changes include what people lovingly refer to as the 'baby belly' and an increase in breast size. During pregnancy there can also be significant physical symptoms that can stop a woman in her tracks, including nausea, vomiting, heartburn, and fatigue, to name a few. Each woman is different in how she experiences these symptoms, which can last a few days, weeks, or the entire duration of her pregnancy. Whatever the duration, physical symptoms and the physical transformation of pregnancy can impact the type of activity a woman engages in and how often or long she can participate in it (e.g., from work, to maintaining her household, to playing sports). A woman's schedule now has to allow for regular monitoring with healthcare providers, which can impact priorities and scheduling. Finally, the physical aspect of labor and delivery as well as the postpartum recovery period, allowing the body to return to homeostasis (or pre-pregnancy state), can be quite uncomfortable and stressful for some women.

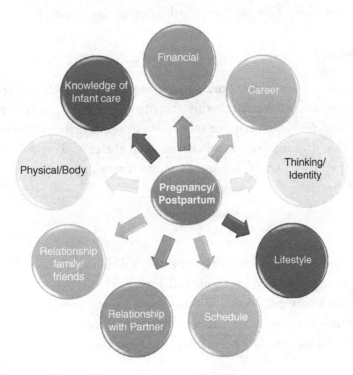

Figure 1.3   Areas of Impact

Relationships and Socialization

It is clear that Dahlia and her husband prioritize their own relationship and their relationships with friends and family. When the baby arrives, all of these relationships are likely to shift in priority as the needs of the baby become the focus of attention. This shift may affect opportunities to socialize as a couple and with friends and family. The quality of relationships may also be affected. It is not uncommon, for example, for both new mothers and new fathers to report a temporary reduction in marital relationship satisfaction, particularly in the early postpartum period. This may be due in part to the challenges that new parents can face when trying to balance the needs of their infant with the activities that help to support and strengthen the marital relationship.

Schedule and Lifestyle

Dahlia has a full schedule filled with full-time work, playing sports, and engaging in activities that she enjoys. With the transition to maternity leave when the baby arrives, Dahlia's lifestyle and schedule will change. She may not be able to participate in sports for a period of time and she will experience changes in her sleep/wake schedule. Instead of her life revolving around her own needs, the baby will become the center of her focus. Although the activities of caring for a new baby may bring Dahlia a sense of joy and accomplishment, she might also experience a sense of loss or an increase in distress as she reduces her involvement in other activities that were important to her or as she and her husband manage the challenge of prioritizing new obligations and responsibilities in day-to-day life.

Thinking/Identity

As Dahlia becomes a new mother, her sense of identify may shift as she incorporates her role as a new parent. Although this transition can be a positive one for some women, others find that they struggle with this change and the sense that important aspects of their identity may not be as central as in the past. This role transition can influence how she views herself, her marriage, her friendships and relationships with others, and her future.

Career

Taking a pregnancy leave from work may affect Dahlia's career. Although some people return to work following a parental leave and hit the ground right where they left off, others may find that the break from their career sets them back from their peers. They may miss an opportunity for promotion or events in the workplace may change the work environment that they return to in unexpected ways.

Financial

With the baby's arrival, there will also be financial changes and Dahlia and her husband may need to make substantial changes to their budget to accommodate increased expenses that come with having a baby, both in the short term (e.g., diapers, strollers, clothes) and long term (e.g., activities, education).

Knowledge of Infant Care

With the arrival of her baby, Dahlia will develop her knowledge and ability to care for her infant. Although she may feel very competent in all areas of her life, with the arrival of her baby, she will be on a new learning curve. She may start out feeling unsure of the best approach to care for her baby. With time, she is likely to become more knowledgeable, comfortable, and confident. For mothers who struggle with anxiety, however, the transition to motherhood can be a time of considerable self-doubt which can add to the distress they may already feel.

What Does Change Have to Do With Anxiety?

The combined influence of the physical/biological, emotional, social, and psychological changes that a pregnant woman or new mother experiences can increase her vulnerability to develop problems with anxiety. This is especially true if she is at higher risk of developing an anxiety disorder because of a personal or family/genetic history of emotional difficulties. Changes in life often lead to uncertainty and uncertainty can result in anxiety (Figure 1.4).

Common Anxious Thoughts or Worries

See Figure 1.5.

What Is Considered 'Normal' Anxiety during Pregnancy and New Motherhood?

Many women in our practice ask us the following question: 'Since I became pregnant and gave birth, my anxiety level has increased … does that mean I am abnormal?' The answer of course is no! There are all sorts of major unknowns and uncertainties when one becomes pregnant or a new mother. Because of these reasons, pregnancy and the postpartum period can be anxiety provoking. Pregnancy and childbirth is a

Figure 1.4 Change, Uncertainty, Anxiety Relationship

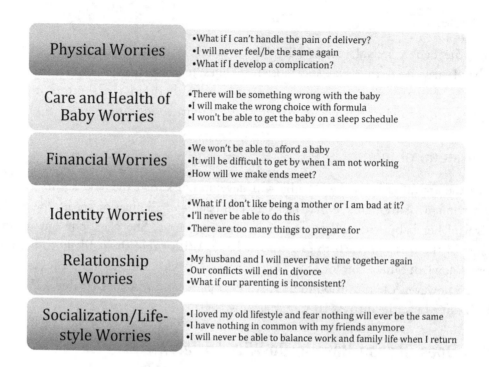

Figure 1.5 Common Worries

time in life that can bring about a number of intense emotional and physical experiences – *both positive and negative.* Grief over the loss of previous roles or freedom to do what you want to do, when you want to do it, is common! Pregnancy and becoming a new parent requires a great deal of adaptation, which can be quite difficult for the average woman and, even more so, for those who have had previous difficulties dealing with anxiety or mood problems.

In 2005, Dr. Wenzel and her colleagues surveyed 150 new mothers about the degree to which they worried about different topics (e.g., relationships, job, finances, appearance, their babies, household duties). They reported that they worried 20–50% of the time. Although their worry did not necessarily take over their lives, it was definitely on their minds a good amount of the time. This level of anxiety is considered *normal* and *to be expected* during pregnancy and postpartum. Figure 1.6 gives a visual representation of this level of 'normal' anxiety during pregnancy and the postpartum.

Anxiety: Range of Intensity

Where one may have been in the 'no anxiety' to 'mild anxiety' range (0–25 range) prior to pregnancy or becoming a new mother, many women experience an increase in anxiety during pregnancy and the postpartum period within the 'mild anxiety' to 'moderate anxiety' range (25–50 range). This range is considered normal given the significant changes that come with preparing for a new baby and adapting once he or she arrives. An interesting way to look at it is that an increase in anxiety is

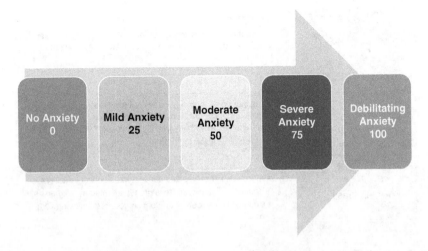

Figure 1.6 Range of Anxiety Severity

considered *adaptive* from an evolutionary perspective because it is *helpful* to be a little more vigilant or preoccupied with the baby to ensure his or her safety. For instance, when the baby begins to cry after being woken up from a nap it alerts you that he or she is in need of something. We are built to respond to the distress of babies by picking them up, giving them a cuddle, changing their diaper, and feeding them. Anxiety is helping us to do this!

However, when anxiety moves from 'moderate' to 'severe' (50–75 range) or beyond (75–100), it is no longer helpful, nor does it serve a practical purpose. In fact, at this level, anxiety can interfere with your ability to care for both your baby and yourself. It is critical that you seek help at this point. Figure 1.7 helps you identify when you might want to seek help when you experience an increase in anxiety.

When Should I Seek Treatment for My Anxiety?

This is certainly an important and sometimes challenging question for a woman to ask herself. We consider three factors when determining whether there is a clinically significant level of anxiety present (Figure 1.7).

If uncertainty remains when questioning whether you should seek treatment, it is always best to make an appointment with your family doctor or another member of your healthcare team to get a professional opinion.

The Many Faces of Women With Anxiety During Pregnancy and New Motherhood

All women experience pregnancy and the postpartum period in their own unique way. Below are a few examples of what anxiety can look like during this time. You may be able to relate to some aspect of each woman's story or perhaps just a detail or

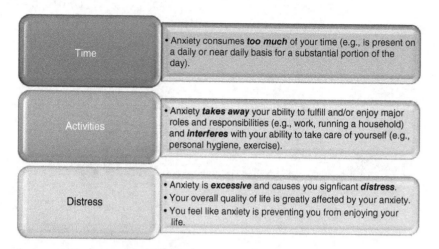

Figure 1.7   Seek Treatment for Anxiety

two from one example. Either way, the purpose of providing these five vignettes is to demonstrate how these women may each have a unique background and story yet share much in common in the experience of their anxiety.

❖ *Cassandra*

Age: 31

Perinatal period: 4 months pregnant

Focus of anxiety: Soon after Cassandra and her husband married two years ago she was overjoyed to learn she was pregnant as she wanted to start a family right away. But when she experienced what the doctors called a 'natural' miscarriage at week ten, her joy quickly turned to devastation. It took Cassandra two years to become pregnant again and now that she is, she fears that she will have another miscarriage or that something will go wrong with the labor and delivery. She is also worried that she will not be able to handle the labor and delivery and that she will have a panic attack during this time. Her husband and doctors reassure her that her healthy pregnancy is progressing as expected, but Cassandra insists on being seen more frequently than needed and receiving more ultrasounds and tests than necessary to reduce her distress with this reassurance.

> I worried about getting pregnant again following my miscarriage and now that I am pregnant, my anxiety has increased. Lately my worry revolves around whether there is/will be something wrong with the baby, so I insist on seeing my doctor weekly and asking for more tests to confirm everything is ok. I also worry that I won't be able to handle labor and delivery and fear that I will have a panic attack during the delivery. I am really worried that this baby won't make it and I won't be able to stop worrying until the baby is born.

❖ *Juanita*

Age: 43

Perinatal period: 8 months pregnant

Focus of anxiety: Juanita and her husband have been married for 12 years and have a six-year-old son. They always wanted another child but put it on hold as Juanita found the postpartum period with her son very difficult, battling symptoms of both anxiety and depression. Even though her family doctor prescribed her an antidepressant during that time, she only found it somewhat helpful and rarely went out with the baby that first year. Juanita and her husband decided that they could no longer delay adding to their family and, as much as she wanted another child, she reluctantly became pregnant again. Having a second child, Juanita is concerned that she will not be able to handle two children once the baby comes. She fears that her family members will not help out or be supportive, although they do live in the same city and she has a good relationship with them. Juanita worries about her depression and anxiety returning, and even being worse than they were before. Further, Juanita is worried that her husband's shift work will prevent him from helping her with the children as much as she needs.

> I remember how much work there was when my first son arrived. Caring for a newborn was all consuming and I felt that I barely got by, especially since I also struggled with postpartum depression and anxiety. Now that my second baby will be arriving shortly, I fear that I will not be able to handle two children. I also worry that the relationship I built with my eldest son will be affected as I will have no quality time with him. I am really worried about the depression and anxiety returning. I don't know how I will manage.

❖ *Zoë*

Age: 23

Perinatal period: 4 weeks postpartum

Focus of anxiety: Zoë has always viewed her mother and much older sister as role models. She has admired her sister and the way she parents her three nieces. Although Zoë's pregnancy was unplanned, she was happy to learn the news as she and her boyfriend had recently moved in together and had a strong relationship. Her pregnancy was smooth, as was her labor and delivery, but as soon as Zoë came home from the hospital, she started to notice a spike in anxiety. She fears that the baby might stop breathing in the night and so she checks the baby multiple times during the night to make sure she is breathing. This has had a considerable impact on Zoë's sleep, further impacting her ability to function. Over the next few weeks she started to fear that she was not being a good mother since this was her first time. She imagined worst-case scenarios like dropping the baby by accident or something bad happening to the baby. As a result, she does not let her boyfriend do much with the baby fearing he won't do it right or properly and something bad will happen. Further, she does not trust anyone aside from her mother, sister, and future mother-in-law who always have advice to give. Zoë seeks reassurance frequently from them to make sure she is doing the right thing. Even though Zoë's anxiety is the most problematic for her, she noticed that her mood is affected as well and she feels down much of the time. She describes her indeterminate anxiety and depression symptoms like a blanket weighing her down that she can never get out from under.

> As soon as I became a mother, I was very anxious about caring for my baby properly and being a good mother. I would check on her multiple times in the night and watch her sleep fearing that she would stop breathing. My sister, mother, and mother-in-law are all great mothers and I find myself asking for their advice in caring for my baby many times throughout the day even when I know the answer. I feel like I don't trust myself or my ability to be a good mother. I worry a lot about something bad happening to my daughter.

❖ *Keesha*

Age: 29

Perinatal period: 3 months postpartum

Focus of anxiety: Keesha viewed herself as self-assured and confident and was never too concerned about what other people thought about her. However, when she started to pull back from work during pregnancy because of her nausea and fatigue she began to fear that others might judge her negatively. This anxiety increased even more when she delivered the baby. She worried that she was not doing the 'right thing' by making the decision to bottle feed half the time and breastfeed the other half. Her self-doubt has had a significant impact on her decisions to go out and do things with the baby in public or receive friends and family in her home. Keesha has noticed that her husband is supportive but disappointed at her decisions to cancel scheduled family visits either in their home or at their family's homes. Her husband seems frustrated that she is constantly seeking reassurance from him and doesn't understand her tendency to avoid or leave these situations.

> Anxiety was never a problem for me in the past, so when I started worrying about what others think of me and my parenting or doing the 'right' thing, it was so upsetting that I started going out less and doubting myself more. Now, I find my mood is down in the dumps too because I have isolated myself. This has taken a toll on my relationship with my husband. He doesn't really seem to understand why this is so hard for me.

❖ *Elizabeth*

Age: 38

Perinatal period: 7 months postpartum

Focus of anxiety: After spending years in school together, Elizabeth and her husband started very demanding careers that they both enjoyed very much. Once they decided that it was time to start a family and the baby arrived, Elizabeth quickly realized how different life became. Taking care of the baby has been all consuming and she was disappointed to learn that she could not do a bit of work during her maternity leave as she had hoped. Further, Elizabeth found herself becoming resentful of her husband, continuing to work in a job he loved with demanding hours that kept him away, while she stayed at home caring for the baby. This resulted in more conflict in their marriage and her anxiety increased as she feared that she would not be able to balance family life and career when she returns to work. Elizabeth also fears she will make the wrong decisions going forward and that she will fail miserably as a mother, wife, and professional.

> Prior to going on maternity leave, my career had been such a big part of my life and something I enjoyed. My husband and I were so happy to welcome our daughter into our lives but I quickly learned how consuming caring for her turned out to be. Multitasking was always something that I was good at but now I find myself not able to accomplish all the things that need to be done in a day. I worry that when I return to work I will not be able to balance family life and work and will make the wrong decisions. I feel really angry with my husband that his life goes on relatively unchanged while I have to take care of everything in the home.

As you can see from these women's stories, a woman can experience a wide variety of anxiety symptoms during pregnancy and new motherhood, but the commonality for all is the distress and life disruption that they experience is anxiety and depression.

Complete Form 1.2 after reflecting on the questions asked about the impact of anxiety on your pregnancy and postpartum period.

Summing It All Up

In this chapter you learned about anxiety and how you may be more vulnerable to experiencing anxiety symptoms during pregnancy and the postpartum period. You gained an awareness of how to distinguish between normal anxiety and clinically significant anxiety during this time, and when you should seek professional help. You may have a better appreciation of how the different domains of your life have been affected by the transition to motherhood, including the biological, psychological, environmental and social factors. You also learned that women may experience anxiety in many different ways. Regardless of how anxiety manifests itself, however, it has the power to cause significant distress and interference in your daily functioning for all. In the next chapter, we turn to examining depression symptoms in pregnancy and the postpartum period.

Self-Reflection: How has Anxiety Affected your Pregnancy and Transition to Motherhood?

Now that you have a better understanding of anxiety, take a few minutes to assess the impact that it has had on you during your pregnancy and/or postpartum period.

1. How has anxiety affected your day-to-day functioning?

_____

_____

_____

2. How has anxiety affected your view of yourself?

_____

_____

_____

3. How has anxiety affected your relationship with your partner or family members?

_____

_____

_____

4. How has anxiety affected your view of your work life and future?

_____

_____

_____

Form 1.2 Self-Reflection

References

Barlow, D. H., & Craske, M. G. (2007). *Mastery of Your Anxiety and Panic: Workbook* (4th ed.). San Antonio, TX: Psychological Corporation.

Steiner, M., Dunn, E., & Born, L. (2003). Hormones and mood: From menarche to menopause and beyond. *Journal of Affective Disorders, 74*, 67–83.

Wenzel, A., Haugen, E. N., Jackson, L. C., & Brendle, J. R. (2005). Anxiety disorders at eight weeks postpartum. *Journal of Anxiety Disorders, 19*, 295–311. doi: 10.1016/j.janxdis.2004.04.001

Chapter 2

Depression During Pregnancy and the Postpartum Period

A Common Co-Occurrence With Anxiety

What Are the 'Baby Blues'? What is Depression?

Why is Depression So Common During Pregnancy and the Postpartum Period?

When Should I Seek Treatment For Depression?

In contrast to the lack of knowledge about anxiety during pregnancy and the postpartum period, the 'baby blues' and postpartum depression are more commonly known by healthcare professionals and the general community. The 'baby blues' (described below) and postpartum depression have been recognized as mental health difficulties since the 1850s (e.g., Marcé, 1858). The baby blues are very common and affect up to 84% of women (O'Hara & Wisner, 2014). Postpartum depression is experienced by 9–19% of women (Woody et al., 2017). Depressive symptoms commonly occur together with anxiety symptoms and the presence of an anxiety disorder may increase the likelihood that someone will develop depressive symptoms as well.

What Are the 'Baby Blues'? Is This Normal?

Symptoms of the 'baby blues' include emotional sensitivity, mild anxiety, irritability, and tearfulness experienced within the first two weeks after a woman delivers her baby (Handley et al., 1980; Yalom et al., 1968). The 'baby blues' are typically short-lived and disappear without need for treatment.

So why does this occur? Researchers investigating the biological causes of the 'baby blues' found that the first days after giving birth overlapped with rapid changes in both hormone levels and brain chemicals that have been associated with depression (e.g., serotonin) (Sacher et al., 2015;

Schiller et al., 2015). These hormonal changes following delivery are thought to trigger postpartum depressive symptoms or 'baby blues' in women whose brains are particularly sensitive (Schiller et al., 2015). The 'baby blues' are far less severe and short-lived compared to postpartum depression. However, it is important to keep in mind that the 'baby blues' may evolve into postpartum depression in some women (Gonidakis et al., 2008).

Depression During Pregnancy and Postpartum Depression

Like the 'baby blues,' postpartum depression is relatively common among women (roughly one in ten). However, unlike the 'baby blues,' postpartum depression is a serious episode of mood symptoms that begins in the days or weeks following the birth of a baby. These symptoms can last from weeks to months and often become worse without treatment. Mothers with postpartum depression may find it increasingly difficult to take care of themselves, their baby, and the things that need to be done throughout the day.

Interestingly, depression *can and does* occur during pregnancy as well. In fact, recent research has shown that in many women diagnosed with postpartum depression, their depression actually started during pregnancy but was not identified or diagnosed earlier. Around one-third of depressive episodes in the postpartum period actually started during the pregnancy. In addition to the biological, and more specifically, hormonal factors that increase a woman's risk of developing postpartum depression, other risk factors include a previous history of depression or other mental health disorders, lack of (or perceived lack of) social support, and marital dissatisfaction (Robertson et al., 2004).

Symptoms of Depression

The term postpartum depression implies that there is something different about depression after childbirth that distinguishes it from depression that occurs at other times in your life. The symptoms of postpartum depression (or depression during pregnancy), however, are identical to those of any other depressive episode outside pregnancy and the postpartum period. Notably, for women with a history of previous postpartum depression in earlier pregnancy (or pregnancies), the risk of having postpartum depression in a subsequent pregnancy increases by 25% (Wisner et al., 2002). In Table 2.1 you will find a list of symptoms that are included in a formal diagnosis of depression (American Psychiatric Association, 2013).

If you suspect or are uncertain whether you might be experiencing some form of depression, it is always best to make an appointment with your family doctor or another member of your healthcare team to get a professional opinion.

Table 2.1 Depression Symptom Checklist

Symptoms of Depression Quick Check

Are you experiencing any of the following symptoms of depression? Clinical depression is defined as follows (American Psychiatric Association, 2013):

☐ Feeling down, depressed, or sad every day, for most of the day for at least two-weeks

Or

☐ Loss of interest or pleasure in things you usually enjoy (such as relationships or hobbies) for at least two-weeks

Plus at least four of the following symptoms present for most of the day every day:

☐ Loss of appetite or increased appetite accompanied by a significant weight loss or gain

☐ Increased sleep (hypersomnia) or decreased or impaired sleep (insomnia, early waking)

☐ Change in activity level from what is normal such as moving very slowly or much faster than is usual for you (e.g., agitation)

☐ Increased fatigue

☐ Difficulty concentrating or making decisions

☐ Excessive feelings of guilt or worthlessness

☐ Suicidal thoughts

Important

If at any time you experience suicidal thoughts or ideation, you should immediately contact your healthcare provider or go to your nearest hospital emergency room.

Screening and Detection of Depression During Pregnancy and the Postpartum Period

As you are reviewing Table 2.1 you may notice that a number of these symptoms are what we would typically associate with pregnancy and the postpartum period and would not necessarily conclude that depression is present. For example, it is quite common for women to have sleep difficulties and feel fatigue when they are pregnant or in the postpartum period when their schedule revolves around the needs of their babies. This brings up two important points. First, practitioners who assess and diagnose depression need to be especially careful when evaluating symptoms that are reported by women who are pregnant or in the postpartum period so as not to over-diagnose these conditions. Second, many women who are suffering from mild depression during pregnancy and the postpartum period remain undetected and treated (Thio et al., 2006) despite the fact that they are in regular contact with health professionals. This is likely because the symptoms of depression tend to be similar to the changes one would expect to be associated with pregnancy and caring for a new baby, including feeling tired, having difficulty sleeping, changes in eating habits and body weight, and stronger emotional reactions. Further, some women are reluctant to disclose how they are feeling and others may not realize that mild depression is present. Another important point is that irritability is sometimes a prominent symptom of postpartum depression, and yet may be less commonly identified as a depressive symptom compared to feelings of sadness, which may delay diagnosis and treatment.

Postpartum Psychosis: An Important Note about a Rare Occurrence

Postpartum psychosis is a rare but frightening occurrence. Only approximately one out of every thousand women are diagnosed with postpartum psychosis, usually within the first few weeks postpartum. Unlike the 'baby blues' or depression, the symptoms in postpartum psychosis may include delusions (i.e., fixed but false beliefs, such as thinking the baby is possessed) and/or hallucinations (e.g., seeing or hearing things that other people cannot see or hear, such as a voice telling them to hurt the baby). Postpartum psychosis is also associated with prominent changes in behavior such as severe agitation and aggression or the opposite, severe slowness (also known as catatonia). Women who have had previous episodes of depression or bipolar disorder have a higher risk of developing depression with psychotic symptoms. Postpartum psychosis is considered a medical emergency and it is important to intervene and ensure support systems are in place to ensure the psychotic symptoms are managed as they emerge.

Understanding Depression: A Multitude of Factors Play a Role

The reasons that contribute to depression can be endless and are not limited to biology. Recall the 'Meet Dahlia' exercise from Chapter 1. This exercise highlighted the fact that having a baby results in many changes in a woman's life, including:

- physical changes
- changes in important relationships (e.g., husband)
- socializing with friends
- changes in lifestyle (e.g., physical exercise, taking vacations)
- financial planning
- priorities in identity (e.g., as a new mother)
- changes in career (e.g., taking time away from work and career goals).

Some of these changes can be challenging adjustments that result in high anxiety, feelings of depression, or both. For instance, a woman's relationship with her partner tends to change from being primarily romantic to primarily a working partnership focused on housework and childcare. A woman may give up paid work, at least temporarily, when having a baby and no longer has time for her own activities. These circumstances can lead to feelings of boredom, isolation, and resentment that can ultimately contribute to symptoms of depression. Further, some women are unprepared for the changes that a baby brings and the amount and type of work involved and may feel angry, ashamed, or sad that they are not living up to societal myths about the 'ideal mother' – this can intensify feelings leading to symptoms of depression.

Another important consideration is that some babies are (normally) more demanding than others and this can also negatively influence the mother. For instance, sleep deprivation can cause mothers to feel overly tired and overwhelmed. Fussy babies can trigger feelings of guilt or shame. All of these aspects are just some of the reasons why family and social support are so important during the early postpartum period and why lack of support is a major risk factor for the development of postpartum depression.

The Many Experiences of Depressive Symptoms during Pregnancy and the Postpartum: Revisiting Our New Mothers and Mothers-to-Be

Every woman is affected differently by the changes that occur during pregnancy and the postpartum period. Below, we revisit our new mothers and the mothers-to-be we introduced in Chapter 1 to understand what is contributing to their depressive symptoms. You may relate to different parts of each woman's story.

❖ *Cassandra*

Cassandra is a 31-year-old woman who is 4 months pregnant with her first child. She is experiencing high anxiety and fear that she will have a miscarriage again or that something bad will happen during her labour and delivery. Her worry and anxiety are all consuming and contributing to her feeling down and depressed. Cassandra's anxiety has also diminished the opportunity to look forward to the arrival of her baby with joy, which has saddened both Cassandra and her husband, as they have wanted to become parents for a long time.

This should be a time of happiness for us. We have waited so long to have a baby but I cannot fully commit to the reality of having a baby as I know that I could miscarry at any point. I am finding it hard to function in the daytime or sleep at night as I worry that I may lose the baby. I am in a constant state of worry that makes it hard to live my life, let alone enjoy it. I don't want to even tell family members I am pregnant let alone start making preparations for the baby.

❖ *Juanita*

Juanita is 43 years old and 8 months pregnant with her second child. She was diagnosed with postpartum depression as well as anxiety after her first child. Although she received treatment in the form of an antidepressant at that time, she only found it somewhat helpful. Juanita has put off having a second child with her husband for fear that she will suffer another depressive episode during her pregnancy and postpartum. Juanita also fears that she will not have the support she needs and that the quality relationship with her older son will end as she will no longer have time with him.

Now that my second baby will be arriving in the next few weeks, I fear that the depression will return as well, especially since I will have two children to care for now instead of just one. I have not set up plans with my support network and don't think I will be able to manage on my own. I also worry that the time with my older son will end and our relationship will suffer.

❖ *Zoë*

Zoë is 23 years old and 4 weeks postpartum with her first child. She has a number of supports to help her during her postpartum. However, Zoë's anxiety prevents her from taking advantage of this as she fears that something bad will happen to the baby. This causes Zoë to over-check the baby and constantly monitor to make sure the baby is safe and happy. This happens at the expense of any time for herself, not to mention, all of the lost sleep while checking on the baby multiple times in the night. As a result, Zoë feels even more fatigued as well as irritable and depressed.

Everyone was so happy when the baby arrived, including me. Caring for a baby is such a big responsibility. I do not want to let anyone down, most importantly my daughter, by missing something or not doing something with her care correctly. I find that staying on top of her care and safety by checking all of the time and doing everything myself, instead of letting others help, has stolen my happiness in being a new mother. I feel like I am not allowed to just be in the moment with my daughter – this has saddened me. I am also so drained and do not feel like myself any more.

❖ *Keesha*

Keesha is 29 years old and 3 months postpartum with her first child. Prior to pregnancy, Keesha would have described herself as self-assured and confident. She never had any difficulties with anxiety or depression in the past so when she started to notice feeling anxious and depressed during her pregnancy she became concerned that something was not right. Her anxiety further increased in the postpartum, when she started to fear other people were judging her ability as a new mother negatively. Keesha started to avoid people more and more as well as confine herself to her home in order to reduce her anxiety about going out and interacting with others. This in turn increased her feelings of depression.

> Anxiety was never a problem for me in the past, so when I started worrying about what others think of me and my parenting or doing the 'right' thing, it was so upsetting that I started going out less and doubting myself more. Now, I find my mood is down in the dumps too because I have isolated myself. This has taken a toll on my relationship with my husband. He doesn't really seem to understand why this is so hard for me.

❖ *Elizabeth*

Elizabeth is 38 years old and 7 months postpartum with her first child. She and her husband were very happy to welcome their daughter into their lives but Elizabeth did not anticipate the incredible transition and adjustment she experienced when moving from full-time work to full-time maternity leave. Elizabeth does not ask for help because she believes that, since she is on maternity leave, she should be the one responsible for the baby at all times. Further, her general perfectionistic approach to completing tasks is making it difficult to find 'me time' to engage in activities that would provide more balance (e.g., exercise, coffee with a friend). As a result, Elizabeth feels depressed, anxious, and hopeless, believing her life will be like this indefinitely.

> Prior to going on maternity leave, my career had been such a big part of my life and something I enjoyed. My husband and I were so happy to welcome our daughter into our lives but I quickly learned how consuming her care turned out to be. Multitasking was always something that I was good at but now I find myself not able to accomplish all the things that need to be done in a day. I worry that when I return to work I will not be able to balance family life and work and fear I will make the wrong decisions. I feel really angry with my husband that his life seems to go on relatively unchanged while I have to take care of the baby and everything in the home.

Take a moment to reflect on the questions in Form 2.1.

Self-Reflection: How Has Depression Affected Your Pregnancy and Transition to Motherhood?

Assess the impact that symptoms of depression might be having on you during your pregnancy and postpartum period.

1. What type of depressive symptoms have you noticed?

Feeling Down

Suicidal thoughts

_____

2. How have symptoms of depression affected your day-to-day functioning?

_____

_____

_____

3. How have symptoms of depression affected your relationship with your partner, friends, or family members?

_____

_____

_____

4. How have symptoms of depression affected your view of your pregnancy, postpartum, and beyond?

_____

_____

_____

Form 2.1 Self-Reflection

If you have been struggling with symptoms of depression, this exercise may have highlighted the toll they have taken on your life. Whether it is the short-lived 'baby blues' or a depressive episode, symptoms of depression can affect your everyday functioning and how you feel about yourself, your baby, and your life in general. The good news is that there are highly effective strategies for targeting your depressive symptoms that we will cover in the next few chapters.

The first step to tackling your depression is identifying the symptoms and understanding their impact, which you have now done. If you have identified that you are experiencing symptoms of depression, we highly recommend checking in with your family doctor or healthcare professional for a more detailed assessment. This is extremely important if you identified feeling suicidal as one of your symptoms.

Summing It All Up

In this section, you have learned about the difference between the 'baby blues' and the symptoms of major depressive disorder. Importantly, although most healthcare practitioners and members of the broader community are often aware of postpartum depression, depressive symptoms can also occur during pregnancy. Because of the degree of interference associated with depressive symptoms for mothers-to-be and new mothers, it is important that you become aware of these symptoms so that you can monitor them over time and target them with strategies from this book as needed. Doing so will give you the best chance of being able to get the help that you need in a timely way.

References

American Psychiatric Association. (2013). *Diagnostic and Statistical Manual of Mental Disorders* (5th ed.). Arlington, VA: Author.

Gonidakis, F., Rabavilas, A. D., Varsou, E., Kreatsas, G., & Christodoulou, G. N. (2008). A 6-month study of postpartum depression and related factors in Athens Greece. *Comprehensive Psychiatry, 49*, 275–282.

Handley, S. L., Dunn, T. L., Waldron, G., & Baker, J. M. (1980). Tryptophan, cortisol and puerperal mood. *British Journal of Psychiatry, 136*, 498–508.

Marcé, L. V. (1858). *Traité de la Folie des Femmes Enceintes, des Nouvelles Accouchées et des Nourrices, et Considérations Médico-légales qui se Rattachent à ce Sujet.* Paris: Baillière.

O'Hara, M. W., & Wisner, K. L. (2014). Perinatal mental illness: Definition, description and aetiology. *Best Practice and Research: Clinical Obstetrics and Gynaecology, 28*, 3–12.

Robertson, E., Grace, S., & Wallington, T. (2004). Antenatal risk factors for postpartum depression: A synthesis of recent literature. *General Hospital Psychiatry, 26*, 289–295.

Sacher, J., Rekkas, R. B., Wilson, A. A., Houle, S., Romano, L., Hamidi, J., . . . Meyer, J. H. (2015). Relationship of monoamine oxidase: A distribution volume to postpartum depression and postpartum crying. *Neuropsychopharmacology, 40*, 429–435.

Schiller, C. E., Meltzer-Brody, S., & Rubinow, D. R. (2015). The role of reproductive hormones in postpartum depression. *CBT Spectrums, 20*, 48–59.

Thio, I. M., Oakley Browne, M. A., & Coverdale, J. H. (2006). Postnatal depressive symptoms go largely untreated: A probability study in urban New Zealand. *Social Psychiatry and Psychiatric Epidemiology, 41*, 814–818.

Wisner, K. L., Parry, B. L., & Piontek, C. M. (2002). Clinical practice: Postpartum depression. *New England Journal of Medicine, 347*, 194–199.

Woody, C. A., Ferrari, A. J., Siskind, D. J., Whiteford, H. A., & Harris, M. G. (2017). A systematic review and meta-regression of the prevalence and incidence of perinatal depression. *Journal of Affective Disorders, 219*, 86–92.

Yalom, I., Tinklenberg, J., & Gilula, M. (1968). *Curative factors in group therapy.* Unpublished manuscript. California: Department of Psychiatry, Stanford University.

Chapter 3

A Cognitive Behavioral Approach for Reducing Symptoms

What is Cognitive Behavioral Therapy?

How Can it Reduce My Anxiety and Depressive Symptoms?

What Are the CBT Strategies That I Can Use to Change How I Feel?

Cognitive behavioral therapy (CBT) is the treatment approach that we are going to be using to tackle your symptoms. CBT is a psychological and behavioral treatment that has been shown to be highly effective for addressing the symptoms of both anxiety and depression, as well as a range of health issues, including chronic pain. In fact, research on the effectiveness of CBT conducted over the past few decades has led to its current status as the *first-line* psychological treatment for anxiety disorders (Butler et al., 2006; Chambless & Ollendick, 2001; Otte, 2011). CBT is based on the idea that your thoughts and your behaviors play an important role in determining how you feel. It is also based on the idea that by choosing how to respond to a particular situation, you have the power to control how you feel. For example, consider the situation of a baby crying in the supermarket and how Keesha (3 months postpartum) and Elizabeth (7 months postpartum) respond differently:

Keesha tended to worry that she wouldn't be able to manage in situations involving her baby and, in particular, worried about how other people viewed her in these situations. When she finally gathered the courage to leave the house to get a few groceries for the week, she was fearful that others would judge her while she was shopping. Keesha's worst nightmare came true: her son started crying when she was waiting in line at the cashier and she had trouble calming him down. Keesha believed that others were staring at her, thinking that she was a bad mother who could not calm her baby. She decided to leave the store without the groceries that she needed for dinner that night. When she left the store, her anxiety was relieved but she then felt defeated for leaving.

Elizabeth found that taking the baby out on errands was becoming a little more challenging now that she was older and taking fewer naps during the day. When Elizabeth stopped at the grocery store to get some food for dinner her daughter was starting to become irritable and Elizabeth could tell that she'd had enough of being out and about for the day. When her baby started to cry while in line at the cashier, Elizabeth took a deep breath, tried her best to soothe her daughter, and reminded herself that this task was almost over and they would soon be on their way home. Elizabeth also noticed that a customer behind her was smiling at her baby and trying to make her laugh, which she thought was kind.

There is no doubt that both Keesha and Elizabeth are going through a challenging situation. However, you can see that each is taking a different approach. Keesha is focused on what other people think of her when her baby is crying and she chooses to escape from the situation to lessen the anxiety that she feels (Figure 3.1). Keesha's thoughts ('Others are staring at me and thinking I am a bad mother') and her behavior (leaving the groceries and racing out of the grocery store) increase the negative impact that anxiety has on her life.

Meanwhile, Elizabeth is focused on the fact that, although this situation is distressing, it is temporary and one that she can manage. She acknowledges that she is doing her best in a challenging situation and is not overly concerned about what other people think. Elizabeth's thoughts ('This is the last task of the day, it is almost over, and we will be on our way home soon') and behavior (taking a deep breath, soothing the baby, noticing others and their positive interactions with her daughter) help her keep her anxiety at a more manageable level and minimize the negative impact her anxiety is having on her day (Figure 3.2).

These examples highlight the important role that both *thoughts* and *behaviors* play in determining how you feel and cope with your anxiety. This is the power of the CBT approach. We all experience distress at times. In many situations, however, we can reduce this distress or increase our sense of being able to cope by choosing how we respond with our thoughts and our behavior. Using CBT you will learn a number of specific strategies to reduce unhelpful thought

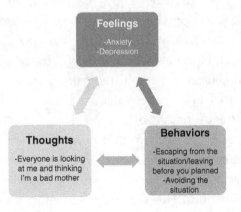

Figure 3.1 Keesha's Example

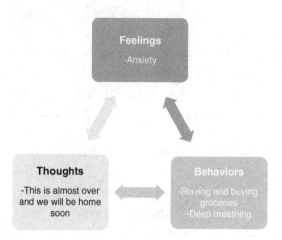

Figure 3.2 Elizabeth's Example

patterns and to improve your behavioral responses to feelings of anxiety and depression.

How CBT Works: Turning Autopilot Off

Many of us go through life on autopilot, not really being present or taking notice of how we respond to the world around us. In this case it may seem like life just 'happens.' Our busy lives too frequently include a packed schedule and trying to get everything on the to-do list done. We are not used to taking a step back and examining our thoughts; we simply have them and they can seem automatic. We also tend not to examine our behaviors and how they influence our thoughts and our feelings. We just live our lives as best we can.

CBT presents us with an opportunity to turn autopilot off by taking a step back. Becoming more aware of the role that our thoughts and behaviors have in our emotional distress can give us the opportunity to *choose* new and more helpful ways of responding. Doing so can give us greater power over how we respond to challenges instead of feeling that life is just 'happening' to us without our having any say in it. In the next section you will learn how to examine your thoughts and shift your perspective. You will also see how your thoughts play an important role in determining how you feel, both emotionally and physically. Finally, you will become aware of the behavioral choices you might be making and, with that awareness, put yourself in a position to make changes that can improve day-to-day functioning, reduce feelings of distress, and ultimately increase confidence. By learning this approach, you will develop the skills to minimize the negative impact that anxiety and depressive symptoms are having on your life. You will have the power to manage (and reduce) your anxiety and depressive symptoms by choosing how you think and respond to situations. However, because you may be working on changing thinking and behavior patterns that have been present for some time, changing them can take time and requires effort. Read on!

What You Put in = What You Get Out!

We are not going to beat around the bush: CBT is a treatment approach that requires your *active* participation in order to be successful. In addition to providing a way to understand your symptoms, CBT involves learning specific strategies designed to reduce your anxiety and depression and enhance your well-being. You will need to set aside time to learn and practice these strategies so that you can experience the benefits of reducing your anxiety and depression and minimize the negative impact they have on your life. This time investment will be worth it given the long-term benefits of CBT. Although CBT and medication for anxiety and depression can be equally beneficial in the short term, studies on the longer-term benefits of treatment show that CBT is associated with lower relapse rates following treatment. Moreover, a number of studies have shown that the benefits of CBT in anxious adults can last for many years following treatment (Borkovec & Costello, 1993; Butler et al., 2006; Durham et al., 2003). In fact, people often find themselves applying these strategies to many areas of their life. This is something we encourage!

Understanding the Connections Between Feelings, Thoughts, and Behavior

An initial step in most CBT programs is to start by increasing your awareness of the symptoms you are experiencing. You have already started this process by learning about the nature of anxiety and depression in Chapters 1 and 2. We have found that just having a better understanding of these symptoms can help women feel more in control and better able to manage their distress. For instance, by understanding what is physically happening to your body when you become anxious (remember the autonomic nervous system/flight or flight system), you might feel less distressed about the symptoms when you experience them because you know what is happening to your body and why.

The next step in a CBT program is to learn about the important connections between symptoms (e.g., anxiety, worry, depressive symptoms), thoughts, and behaviors. With this information, you can then use CBT strategies that are tailored specifically to target thoughts and behaviors that might be adding to your distress.

Another important component of any CBT program is called *psychoeducation*. Psychoeducation is just a fancy word for learning more about the nature of your disorder or difficulty – something you have been doing thus far with Chapters 1 and 2. To begin, take a look at the CBT model (Figure 3.3).

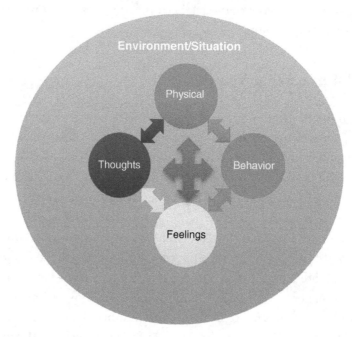

Figure 3.3 The CBT Model

Within the CBT model you can see that our feelings, thoughts, behaviors, and physical symptoms all occur within our larger environment. They are also interconnected, which means that if you change one it has the possibly to affect and change the others. For example, if you change your behavior (e.g., getting up and having a shower as opposed to staying in bed), it has the potential to change how you think (e.g., I can do this), how you feel (e.g., less depressed, more hopeful), and the physical sensations (e.g., less fatigue, more energy) you experience. The different connections can interact to produce more anxiety and distress. They can also interact to create a more helpful or adaptive way of responding and as a result, less anxiety and depression. As you start to bring awareness to your own thoughts and behaviors in situations that bring about anxiety, you will be able to change how your think, behave, and ultimately, feel. The examples below illustrate how these interacting connections may play out in daily life for the women who were introduced in Chapter 1.

How to Apply the CBT Model

Reflect over the past week on the experiences that brought about significant anxiety or depression and consider them in relation to the CBT model in Figure 3.3. Your goal in practicing applying the CBT model is to identify the different components of your experience of anxiety or depression in recent situations. Although it may seem surprising that we want you to spend time monitoring distressing experiences (and our clients often tell us they know them all too well!), we know that doing so can often be extremely enlightening. Remember, these experiences are often automatic. They can happen so fast that you may be unaware of the components that are adding to you distress. Careful monitoring of situations that elicit anxiety or depression in this unique way slows this process down, giving you the best chance to identify the parts of the experience that you are going to want to change later in this program.

Working With the CBT Model

To complete the CBT model worksheet (Form 3.1), start by thinking about a time in the past week when you were feeling anxious or depressed. Briefly describe the situation you were in and then identify the feelings you experienced in that moment – there may have been more than one feeling. Identify the severity/intensity of the feeling of on a scale from 0 to 100, where 0 indicates that the feeling is not at all severe and 100 is the most severe. Use Figure 3.4 and Keesha's example as a guide.

Next, what physical sensations did you experience (e.g., increased heart rate, rapid breathing, feeling lightheaded)? After that, write down the thought(s) that you had in the situation. There may have been more than one. Finally, what did you do? Did you stay in the situation? Or leave it?

Keesha's example

Environment/Situation: Wednesday 3 p.m., in line at grocery store and baby starts crying

Feeling: Anxiety

Severity/Intensity: 85

Physical: Heart racing, sweating, short of breath, tension

Thoughts: Everyone is looking at me and thinking I am a bad mother

Behaviors: Avoid looking at others, abandon the groceries, escape the grocery store

Environment/Situation:_____

Feeling:_____

Severity/Intensity:_____

Physical:_____

Thoughts:_____

Behaviors:_____

Environment/Situation:_____

Feeling:_____

Severity/Intensity:_____

Physical:_____

Thoughts:_____

Behaviors:_____

Environment/Situation:_____

Feeling:_____

Severity/Intensity:_____

Physical:_____

Thoughts:_____

Behaviors:_____

Form 3.1 CBT Model Worksheet

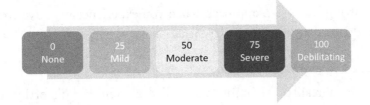

Figure 3.4 Severity of Anxiety

CBT Strategies: The Basics

Once you have learned to identify the individual components of your experience in situations involving anxiety or depressive symptoms, and have a good understanding of the connections between these components, the next step is to develop the skills to change the components of these situations that may be contributing to your distress. In particular, CBT strategies are the tools you will use to target the cognitive and behavioral components of the CBT model. The specific strategies that you will learn are presented in Part II, although we begin here by discussing the basic rationale for these strategies.

Cognitive Strategies

The goal of cognitive strategies is to shift your perspective or way of *thinking* about a situation to be more helpful or realistic. Day to day, the average person does not spend too much time thinking about what their thoughts are at any given time. Most people are more focused on getting their 'to-do' lists done or following through with their responsibilities and may not even be aware of specific thoughts that play an important role in their emotional experiences. For instance, Juanita might be having a day where she is accomplishing what she hoped to. However, because she is thinking about the future when her second baby is born and experiencing thoughts such as 'I will never be able to handle all of the tasks that need to be done,' her anxiety level might be particularly high, causing her to cancel a coffee date with a friend, and subsequently influencing her mood to become more depressed. By becoming more aware of your thoughts, you can take control of how you feel and respond. This is the basic premise of cognitive strategies pioneered by Aaron Beck (Beck et al., 1979) and Albert Ellis (Ellis & Harper, 1961).

Once you become aware of your thoughts, you can examine them to see whether they are realistic or helpful in a given situation. We all have our own unique way of perceiving the world, influenced by our past experiences and our personality. Certain styles of thinking, also known as *cognitive distortions* or *thinking errors*, can increase the likelihood of experiencing negative emotions, including feelings of anxiety, unhappiness, and depression. Some common types of cognitive distortions or thinking errors have been identified (Barlow, Brown, & Craske, 1994; Burns, 1980) and in the next chapter we have modified them to be representative of pregnancy and the postpartum context.

In the chapters that follow, you will become skilled at shifting your thoughts using the following three-step approach when you experience negative emotions such as anxiety or depression in a particular situation.

1. Step back and examine your thoughts.
2. Identify an unrealistic thought (also called a cognitive distortion or thinking error).
3. Consider ways of interpreting or thinking about the situation that are more realistic or helpful.

Cognitive strategies are an important part of any CBT treatment plan, and they are even more powerful when combined with behavioral strategies.

Behavioral Strategies

Behavioral strategies aim to change what you do in response to a situation in which you experience distress. Behavioral change requires *effort* because old habits are hard to break. However, the key to better coping is to keep an open mind and to be willing to experiment with new behaviors or responses to specific situations. You will find that changing your behaviors in a strategic way will change how you think as well as how you feel. This brings us to the next step in the process: Setting goals.

Setting Goals for CBT during Pregnancy and the Postpartum Period

It is very important to have clearly defined goals before starting a new treatment. Having specific goals can help clarify what you want to achieve and allows you to determine when you have been successful in applying the strategies that you have learned in CBT. It is important to set realistic and attainable goals for treatment. Take, for example, someone who wants to treat her chronic pain. CBT has been shown to be a very effective treatment for this condition. However, if someone begins a CBT for chronic pain program with the goal of eliminating pain completely they will be sadly disappointed as this goal is *unrealistic*. A more realistic goal would be to reduce the *severity* of the pain, the *frequency* of flare-ups, the *distress* associated with it, and the *interference* that pain is presently having in her life.

The same is true for anxiety. It is not a realistic possibility to eliminate the symptoms of anxiety altogether. A more realistic goal would be to reduce the severity of your symptoms, the negative impact they have on your life in terms of interference and distress, and the frequency of anxiety symptoms. Prior to setting your goals, have a look at the treatment goals that were set by Cassandra, Juanita, Zoë, Keesha, and Elizabeth below:

Cassandra's CBT Treatment Goals

Goal 1: To feel less anxious and more confident about this pregnancy and delivery.

Goal 2: To reduce the amount of reassurance seeking I engage in.

Goal 3: To spend more time enjoying my pregnancy and looking forward to the arrival of the baby.

Juanita's CBT Treatment Goals

Goal 1: To develop a plan to help me continue to have a relationship with my eldest son when the baby comes.

Goal 2: To develop a plan before the baby arrives for getting the support and help I will need from others.

Goal 3: To learn ways to relax my body when anxiety hits.

Zoë's CBT Treatment Goals

Goal 1: To feel more confident about my abilities as a mother and the choices I make.

Goal 2: To reduce the amount of checking and reassurance seeking I engage in.

Goal 3: To take better care of myself so that I can better care for my baby.

Keesha's CBT Treatment Goals

Goal 1: To not worry so much about what others think of me and my parenting.

Goal 2: To go out more with the baby.

Goal 3: To have people visit in my home more often.

Elizabeth's CBT Treatment Goals

Goal 1: To stop striving for perfection and acknowledge when good enough is good enough.

Goal 2: To engage in more of my own activities to feel more balanced as a person.

Goal 3: To work on improving the relationship with my husband.

Your CBT Treatment Goals

Goal 1:_____

_____

Goal 2:_____

_____

Goal 3:_____

_____

Summing It All Up

CBT is an evidence-based psychological treatment based on the idea that you can change how you feel by changing how you think and behave in response to a given situation. CBT provides a framework or model for understanding your symptoms as it breaks them down into components: physical symptoms, thoughts, feelings, and behaviors. These components interact to create your response to a situation. CBT involves a set of skills that you will learn to target unhelpful or unrealistic thoughts (also known as cognitive distortions or thinking errors) and problematic behaviors that contribute to your distress. It takes effort to develop these skills, but once you learn them, you can use these strategies to address anxiety and depression and greatly improve your quality of life.

References

Barlow, D. H., Brown, T. A., & Craske, M. G. (1994). Definitions of panic attacks and panic disorder in the DSM-IV: Implications for research. *Journal of Abnormal Psychology, 103,* 553–564.

Beck, A. T., Rush, J., Shaw, B., & Emery, G. (1979). *Cognitive Therapy of Depression.* New York, NY: Guilford Press.

Burns, D. D. (1980). *Feeling Good: The New Mood Therapy.* New York, NY: Morrow.

Borkovec, T. D., & Costello, E. (1993). Efficacy of applied relaxation and cognitive-behavioural therapy in the treatment of generalized anxiety disorder. *Journal of Consulting and Clinical Psychology, 61,* 611–619. doi: 10.1037/0022-006X.61.4.611

Butler, A. C., Chapman, J. E., Forman, E. M., & Beck, A. T. (2006). The empirical status of cognitive-behavioral therapy: A review of meta-analyses. *Clinical Psychology Reviews, 26,* 17–31. doi: 10.1016/j.cpr.2005.07.003

Chambless, D. L., & Ollendick, T. H. (2001). Empirically supported psychological interventions: Controversies and evidence. *Annual Review of Psychology, 52,* 685–716. doi: 10.1146/annurev.psych.52.1.685

Durham, R. C., Chambers, J. A., MacDonald, R. R., Power, K. G., & Major, K. (2003). Does cognitive-behavioural therapy influence long-term outcome of generalized anxiety disorder? An 8–14 year follow-up of two clinical trials. *Psychological Medicine, 33,* 499–509. doi: 10.1017/S003329170200707

Ellis, A., & Harper, R. A. (1961). *A Guide to Rational Living.* Englewood Cliffs, NJ: Prentice-Hall.

Otte, C. (2011). Cognitive behavioral therapy in anxiety disorders: Current state of the evidence. *Dialogues in Clinical Neuroscience, 13,* 413–421.

Part II

CBT for Anxiety and Depression

A Step-By-Step Approach to Treatment

Chapter 4

Increasing Your Awareness and Understanding Your Triggers

Why Is Awareness So Important?

How Do I Break Down My Experience with Anxiety and Depression?

How Do I Evaluate My Thoughts?

These next six chapters in Part II are referred to as *step-by-step treatment* chapters. Here, you will learn the 'active ingredients' of cognitive behavioral therapy (CBT), namely the tools, skills, and strategies that are used to manage your anxiety and depression. The first step in the CBT approach is to increase your *awareness*. By becoming aware and having a good understanding of what contributes to the problem – in this case anxiety and depression – we put ourselves in a better position to be able to treat it more effectively. It is certainly common for people who are having difficulty with anxiety and depression to report that they *always* feel anxious or depressed. You may be able to relate to this or perhaps your experience is different, in that you notice your anxiety increases in certain situations or your depression worsens at certain times of the day. Either way, it is important to begin by monitoring your experiences with anxiety and depression more closely using a CBT-based approach.

Recall the cognitive behavioral model (CBT model) that was first introduced in Chapter 3 (refer to Figure 4.1). When you experience an increase in anxiety, depression, or another negative feeling, a number of factors can contribute to your symptoms. These include the environment or situation you are in, the thoughts you experience, the behaviors or actions you engage in, and the physical sensations you experience (or your 'biology').

Consider an example from Keesha's experience. She acknowledges that her anxiety increases every time the phone rings but might not recognize that her anxiety increases because she fears it could be 'someone calling and wanting to visit,' which might lead to people coming over and judging her ability to care for her baby in a negative way.

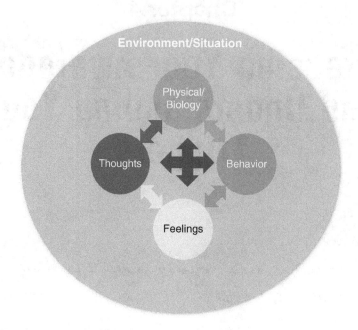

Figure 4.1 Cognitive Behavioral Model

Similarly, Juanita notices that when she looks in the mirror she experiences an increase in anxiety. However, in this described anxious moment she is not able to make the connection that her very pregnant appearance is indicative that her second baby is arriving soon and that she has not set up the help she needs from her social network for when she has two children to care for.

In Elizabeth's case, she notices that her anxiety and depression both increase in the morning when her husband leaves for work. In this example, Elizabeth may have a lack of awareness with respect to how her thoughts and behaviors are contributing to her distress. Specifically, she might have had the thought: 'I should be able to take care of the baby today and take care of cleaning the house without help, and yet I am afraid that I will not be able to.' This thought contributes to her increasing anxiety about the upcoming day. Moreover, if she has trouble in being assertive and asking her husband to take care of the baby after work or on the weekend, she will have no time to rest or engage in the activities that bring balance to her life which might, in turn, lead to increased feelings of depression.

As you can see, a number of factors can contribute to your anxiety and depression at any one time, from situations and thoughts to behaviors and physical sensations/ biology. By becoming *aware* of all of these components in any given situation, you put yourself in a better position to make strategic changes using specific cognitive and behavioral strategies that you will be learning in the next chapters.

Bringing Awareness Using the Thought-Monitoring Form

We break down experiences of anxiety and depression by using a tool called the *thought-monitoring form*. This form allows you to document the details of your anxious or depressed experience: from the situation you are in and the thoughts you have, to the feelings and physical sensations you notice. Writing down your experience not only allows you to become aware of and break down all of the factors that are contributing to your anxiety and depression, but also allows your brain to process and evaluate this information in a different, more helpful way.

Over the next week, use the thought-monitoring form (Form 4.1) to record the times when you notice an increase in anxiety, depression, or another negative emotion. Here you will describe the situation you were in (e.g., what day of the week and time of day it was, who you were with, where you were), the feelings you had (e.g., anxiety, depression, guilt, shame, stress), and their severity (0 = not present; 100 = severe). You will also document the physical sensations you were having (e.g., heart racing, feeling hot or sweaty, dizzy/lightheaded, short of breath), and the thoughts that you had at that time (e.g., what was going through your mind, what you thought of the situation). Leave the 'Thinking Errors' column empty for the moment.

Situation	Feelings (0–100)	Physical Sensations	Thoughts	Thinking Errors
What day of the week and time of day was it? Where were you? Who were you with? What were you doing?	What were you feeling? How intense was each feeling you had, rated from 0 to 100 (0 = not at all; 100 = totally debilitating)?	What did you notice in your body? Heart racing, shortness of breath, feeling hot or sweaty, chest pressure, lightheaded, dizzy?	What were your thoughts? What did you think about what was happening? What was going through your mind?	Reflecting on your thoughts, can you identify any thinking errors?

Form 4.1   Thought-Monitoring Form

Please note that you will complete a thought-monitoring form *after* the situation has occurred and *not during* the situation. For example, Elizabeth waited for her husband to leave for work before she sat down to complete a thought-monitoring form. Use Elizabeth's and Juanita's forms as examples (Forms 4.2 and 4.3).

Situation	Feelings (0–100)	Physical Sensations	Thoughts	Thinking Errors
Wednesday morning, watching my husband get ready for work as I am having breakfast and feeding our daughter	Anxious (70) Distant (60) Frustrated (70) Depressed (70)	■ Heart racing ■ Sweating ■ Shortness of breath ■ Fatigue	■ I am the one on maternity leave, so it's my responsibility to take care of the baby and the household. I should be able to do it all and be happy but I'm not sure I'll be able to ■ He gets to go to the work, something we both love, and continue with his weekly 'guys' night out.' I am stuck and will never find balance again! ■ I am so tired and frustrated – I must have made the wrong decision to have a family	■ Should statements ■ Catastrophizing ■ Fortune telling/ jumping to conclusions ■ Emotional reasoning

Form 4.2 Thought-Monitoring Form: *Elizabeth's Example*

Situation	Feelings (0–100)	Physical Sensations	Thoughts	Thinking Errors
Saturday morning, getting ready for the day. Looking in the mirror and seeing my 8-month baby bump	Anxious (90) Overwhelmed (80) Worried (75) Sad (65)	■ Dizzy ■ Lightheaded ■ Nauseous ■ Unreal	■ I don't know if I will be able to handle my life with another baby. I sometimes feel like I can barely manage as it is ■ What if do not get the help I need and I have another postpartum depression? ■ I am upset with myself for having these feelings. I should be able to cope	■ Fortune telling/jumping to conclusions ■ Catastrophizing ■ Negative filter ■ Should statements

Form 4.3 Thought-Monitoring Form: *Juanita's Example*

Evaluating Your Thoughts – The 'C' in CBT

Do you believe that all your thoughts are accurate and true? Many people never stop to consider this question. It may be surprising to learn the truth that *not all thoughts are facts*. We as human beings have hundreds of thoughts each day. Our thoughts can be classified as either *automatic* or *intentional*. Automatic thoughts are thoughts that we have *no control* over. They just appear, whether we like it or not. Often, we are not even aware of our automatic thoughts because they can happen so quickly.

Unlike automatic thoughts, we *do have control* over our intentional thoughts. An example of an intentional thought is, 'What am I going to make for dinner?' and 'I have cheese and eggs in the fridge, maybe I will make an omelette.' What both automatic thoughts and intentional thoughts do have in common is that they are not always accurate. *Thinking errors*, also known as *cognitive distortions*, are what we label thoughts that are inaccurate or false. You may also be surprised to learn that the average person makes *several* thinking errors every day regardless of whether or not that person has problems with anxiety or depression.

Take the following as a common example in northern climates. Imagine your alarm clock wakes you up on a Monday morning in mid-January. You notice that there are blizzard conditions outside. It would not be uncommon (and certainly understandable) for the average person to think something along the lines of: 'It's the beginning of a work week, there is a blizzard outside and I am still tired. This is going to be a horrible day, I might as well just stay in bed.' Is this true? Although, you may certainly appreciate the difficulty of the situation, this is an example of a *thinking error*. True, it is the start of a work week. It is mid-January, the lovely spring season is a long way off, and there is a blizzard outside. However, nobody knows whether it will be a *horrible* day and one that warrants remaining in bed. Specifically, this is an example of a thinking error that would be categorized under 'catastrophizing' and 'fortune telling.'

See Table 4.1 for common categories of thinking errors that are experienced during pregnancy and the postpartum period along with some examples. As you read through the list of thinking error categories, you may find you can relate to some more than others. Use Form 4.4 to write down three or four of the thinking error categories that you feel you relate to the most and jot down a few examples of your own thinking errors that would fit under this category. Use Elizabeth's and Juanita's entries as an example.

Table 4.1 Common Thinking Errors During Pregnancy and the Postpartum Period

Thinking Error	Definition	Examples
Probability overestimation	You overestimate the likelihood of something (bad) happening	■ There will be something wrong with my baby ■ If my baby doesn't latch right away I won't be able to breastfeed ■ I won't be able to handle having a new baby ■ This will never end (e.g., crying)
Catastrophizing	You view the outcome of an event or situation in the worst possible way or as a major disaster	■ My baby is crying uncontrollably in the grocery store. People will think I am a terrible mother ■ My husband and I are arguing more; this will lead to a divorce ■ My baby's sleep will never get any better and so I will never be able to get a good night's sleep again
All or nothing/ black or white	You see things in black-and-white categories. If your performance as a mother falls short of perfect, you see yourself as a total failure	■ If I am not able to breastfeed, I will be a failure as a mother ■ If I can't get my baby to stop crying, I am a terrible parent
Personalizing	You attribute full responsibility of a situation or outcome to yourself	■ It is my fault if my baby gets sick or if my baby does not reach a developmental milestone on time ■ If there is something wrong with my baby it means that I did not take enough care of myself during pregnancy
Negative filter/ discounting the positives	You see only the negative aspects of a situation and reject positive experiences by insisting they 'don't count' for some reason or another	■ I only had time to pick up the groceries but I didn't get to the post office as I had planned or to the drugstore because I couldn't calm the baby...what a waste of a day ■ Others have been telling me about how many sacrifices I will have to make when the baby arrives – I'm not going to enjoy my new life

(Continued)

Table 4.1   (Cont.)

Thinking Error	Definition	Examples
Fortune telling/ jumping to conclusions	You predict the future, anticipating that things will go badly before you enter into a situation, and believe it to be true	■ I won't be able to handle my labor and delivery ■ I won't know what to do/how to care for my baby when he/she arrives ■ I will be completely overwhelmed when I go back to work and have no work/family balance ■ I will choose the wrong childcare for my baby
Mind reading	Believing that you know how someone else is feeling or what that person is thinking without any evidence	■ Everyone must be watching me and thinking how incompetent I am as a mother ■ Others will be judging me and wondering why my baby needs a soother at this age
Should statements	You try to motivate yourself with 'shoulds' and 'should nots' by applying rigid rules or expectations for yourself or others. If you then struggle to follow these rules, the emotional consequences can be guilt and anger. 'Musts' and 'oughts' are also common terms	■ I should be able to keep the house clean, prepare dinner, and look after my baby every day ■ I should be able to do more/as much as I used to before the baby came ■ My husband must know how tired I am, but is refusing to help me out
Emotional reasoning	Believing that something is true because it feels true: 'I feel it, therefore it must be true'	■ I feel guilty for starting back at work and putting my child in daycare so it must mean I am a bad mother ■ I am not enjoying parenthood all the time . . . I often feel impatient, anxious, and depressed so it must mean that I made the wrong decision to have a family

My Common Thinking Errors

Juanita's Example
Thinking Error: All or Nothing

1. I will be completely unable to handle two children.

2. My good relationship with my older son will end as I will have no quality time with him.

3. No one will be there to help me when the baby arrives.

Elizabeth's Example
Thinking Error: Should Statement and Catastrophizing

1. I should be able to do all of the childcare and housework since I am on maternity leave.

2. I am stuck and will never find balance again.

Thinking Error:

1._____

2._____

3._____

Thinking Error:

1._____

2._____

3._____

Thinking Error:

1._____

2._____

3._____

Thinking Error:

1._____

2._____

3._____

Form 4.4   Lists of My Common Thinking Errors

You are now in a position to return to your thought-monitoring form and complete the final column labeled 'Thinking Errors.' Here, we want you to evaluate the thoughts you wrote down in the thought-monitoring form and consider which of the thinking errors would apply. Similar to Elizabeth's and Juanita's examples, if you determine that some or all of the thoughts you wrote down are not accurate, what category do you think captures the essence of your thought? Please keep in mind that a single thought could easily fall into more than one category.

Take Elizabeth's thought, 'I am so tired and frustrated. I must have made the wrong decision to have a family.' This can fit into more than one category, including *emotional reasoning,* as she is drawing a conclusion based on how she *feels* in that moment, as well as *catastrophizing,* as she is evaluating the situation in an *extreme* way (having a family versus not having a family).

It is also important to note that the thoughts you wrote down on your thought-monitoring form may not *all* be inaccurate or fall within a thinking error category. This happens all the time. People with anxiety and depression have a higher frequency of thinking errors, especially in situations when anxiety and depression levels are high. However, we all continue to experience accurate thoughts, which may in fact appear on your thought-monitoring form too.

Activity: Getting to Know Your Thoughts

Over the next week, try to complete three or four thought-monitoring forms based on situations where you noticed an increase in your anxiety, depression, or another negative emotion. Once complete, start reading Chapter 5 on Tackling Thinking Errors: Three Cognitive Strategies. There you will learn how to correct the thinking errors you identified in your thought-monitoring forms and work toward more balanced thinking.

Summing It All Up

Many of the thoughts we have each day are *automatic* or occur without our intending to think them. These thoughts can be distinguished from *intentional* thoughts that we are aware of and yet *both* types of thoughts can have a significant impact on our emotions and behavior. Although many of our daily thoughts are accurate and helpful, from time to time we all experience thoughts that contain *thinking errors.* These thoughts might contain information that is inaccurate or unhelpful or may not reflect *all* aspects of a particular situation. These are the thoughts that are the most likely to have a negative impact on emotion and behavior. Becoming more aware of thoughts that contain thinking errors, whether they are automatic or intentional, is a critical first step in identifying the thoughts we want to change. The more we monitor our thoughts, the more aware we are of the thinking errors we make.

Chapter 5

Tackling Thinking Errors

Three Cognitive Strategies

I Have Identified My Thinking Errors, Now What Do I Do?

Is it Normal to Still Feel Anxious and Depressed, Even With A More Balanced Thought?

How Long Do I Have to Practice These Cognitive Strategies For?

In Chapter 4, you learned that the first step in taking a cognitive behavioral therapy (CBT) approach is to become more *aware* of what influences your anxiety, depression, and other negative feelings. By becoming more aware of what contributes to your experience of anxiety and depression, you are in a better position to target and treat these symptoms strategically. You were also introduced to a tool called the thought-monitoring form, which allowed you to break down your anxious or depressed experience in a way that allows greater awareness. We cannot stress the importance of this first step, as the information in the *'Thought'* column of your thought-monitoring form is what you will work with in this chapter.

Now that you have completed several thought-monitoring forms and identified a number of your thinking errors, the goal is to create more *balanced* and *accurate* thoughts. Using the three cognitive strategies introduced in this chapter, you will learn how to shift your thinking patterns from negative thinking errors that lead to feelings of anxiety and depression to a more helpful and balanced way of thinking. Shifting your thinking pattern in this way is a process that you will go through by practicing the strategies – one thought at a time. This process is also called *cognitive restructuring*.

Remember, *everybody* makes thinking errors regardless of whether they suffer from anxiety or depression. The important difference, though, is that individuals who do not have elevated anxiety or depression tend to identify thoughts that contain thinking errors more quickly and then correct them more easily, at times even automatically, as they consider other ways of viewing a situation. Alternatively, they will have a lower ratio of thinking errors to more balanced thoughts overall. Finally, individuals who have *higher* levels of anxiety or depression are more likely to *believe* that these thinking errors are true. As a result, those suffering from anxiety and depression are more likely to pull the covers over their head and stay in bed in the case of the example from Chapter 4 where they wake up to a blizzard outside. The average person, however, is much more likely to get out of bed and have a shower after changing the thinking error to something along the lines of:

> True, there is a blizzard outside, it is Monday morning, and it is January, all of which I do not like. However, I am meeting my friend Heather for lunch and I am going to watch my nephew's basketball game in the evening. Maybe it won't be such a bad day after all.

Notice that the thought changed from a negative thinking error to one that is more *balanced and accurate*. It is not overly positive, nor is it unrealistic, such as the following thought: 'This is going to be a fantastic day.' Although this is a positive thought, it is unrealistic and something your brain simply will not accept – and rightly so. It sees the blizzard outside and acknowledges that it is a Monday in the month of January – all factors that this particular person does not like.

The three cognitive strategies we present in this chapter will allow you to take *one thinking error at a time* and work on finding an alternative, more balanced, or more helpful thought. We offer three different cognitive strategies as you may prefer one strategy over another or find one strategy more helpful than another in relation to a specific thinking error. Changing thoughts from negative and inaccurate, to ones that are balanced and accurate, is a key strategy in CBT. Thoughts are very powerful. If you can change your thoughts, you have the ability to change how you feel and, change how you respond (e.g., your behavior).

Cognitive Strategy #1: The Best Friend Technique

Imagine the following situation: You have an early-morning appointment at the doctor's office for your baby's first immunization. You try your best to prepare in advance by packing your diaper bag, showering the evening before, and getting your outfit ready for the next morning. Unfortunately, the baby is up several times in the night and you end up only getting a few hours of sleep. You sleep through your alarm the next morning and get up in a panic, waking your baby (who is not happy with this) in an effort to hustle out the door. You arrive a half-hour late and notice that the receptionist is not pleased that you are late or the fact that you forgot your health insurance information. What would you think in this situation? Would you be critical of yourself or understanding and compassionate? If you are like many of the new mothers we have worked with, you might be thinking in a negative or self-critical way about yourself.

Now imagine that this has happened to another mother, to your best friend, or to someone else that you care about. What would you think of her? Would your thoughts be as critical or would you be more understanding and compassionate? Even though it is the *same situation*, chances are you may have two different judgments, one for yourself and one for the other mother. As human beings we tend to judge ourselves more critically and in an unsympathetic way, while judging others with more compassion and with more reasonable standards. For instance, evaluating yourself in this situation, you might be less likely to discount the long night spent caring for the baby resulting in little sleep and the stressful circumstance of waking the baby and rushing out the door. Instead, negative thoughts may include 'They are going to think I am a lazy mother' or 'This is unacceptable – I should always be on time.' On top of already feeling upset, you might be more likely to criticize yourself with thoughts such as 'I can never get anything right' or "I can't even get to a doctor's appointment. What is wrong with me?' These thoughts are thinking errors because they do not reflect all aspects of the situation and they are certainly not helpful as they compound your stress and lead to a host of negative feelings.

On the other hand, evaluating another mother in this example, you are more likely to understand that she had the best intentions by trying to prepare the night before, having a shower and preparing her clothes in advance, getting her diaper bag ready, and setting her alarm. However, you might also have been aware that there were some significant circumstances that were out of her control and that contributed to her late arrival, including the fact that the baby was up multiple times and she had very little sleep. Further, having to wake up the baby, who was not pleased, was a stressful situation, not to mention the distress of knowing that she would be late.

A way to balance these thoughts or to make them more accurate or helpful is to imagine what you would say to someone else if she was in your situation, such as another mother or your best friend. Would you be as critical or unfair in your evaluation? Would you call her lazy? Of course not! You would be more likely to say something along the lines of:

> You take these appointments very seriously and you tried your best to get to the appointment on time. Your efforts of preparing the night before really show that. You need to remember that your baby was up several times last night and you had a terrible night of sleep. It is hard to function with this amount of sleep when you do not have to be somewhere on time and it is even more difficult when you have to be

at a morning appointment. You did your best to get to the doctor's office on time.

Now it is your turn to use the 'best friend' technique. Select one of the situations that you recorded in your thought-monitoring form that was associated with heightened feelings of anxiety or depression. The instructions for the form are below. Use Keesha's and Juanita's examples as a guide (Forms 5.1 and 5.2).

Instructions for the 'Best Friend' Technique

Step 1: Using a completed thought-monitoring form, write down the details of the situation.

Step 2: Write down one (or more) identified thinking errors from that situation and place them in the '*What Are My Thoughts In This Situation?*' column.

Step 3: Picture another mother or your best friend. Write down what you might say to her in the '*What Would I Think Or Say To My Best Friend Or Another Mother In This Situation?*' column.

Step 4: Reread the content in the second column, *over and over* again, every day. These are your new balanced, more helpful, or more accurate thoughts!

What Are My Thoughts In This Situation?	*What Would I Think Or Say To My Best Friend Or Another Mother In This Situation?*
1. I am so incompetent. (*emotional reasoning*)	1. You are doing the best you can in this challenging situation and are *not* incompetent. You can't control when a baby will cry, because that's what babies do, they cry!
2. Everyone I talked to at the beginning of class, when my son was happy, now sees me as 'falling apart' and wants to steer clear of me. (*mind reading*)	2. Other mothers probably understand what it is like to be in a challenging situation like this and are more likely to be sympathetic rather than critical. Remember, there were a couple of mothers who asked if you needed your diaper bag or if they could help. Other mothers might just be giving you some room to 'work with' your baby to calm him. You know how you like your space to try to calm your baby down. Others might feel the same way and are giving you space.
3. This was an awful experience that I can't handle. I will never come back or go to other public places with him if I can help it! (*catastrophizing*)	3. It is important to remember that you were enjoying yourself tremendously in the first half of the class and connecting with some of the mothers before your son started crying. If you do not go back you might miss out on a good time. You should also remember all of the times that you have gone out with your son and have been able to calm him when he has started to cry. Plus, in spite of the fussy fit, you were able to handle the situation. You continued with the class and were eventually able to soothe your son.

Form 5.1 Best Friend Technique: *Keesha's Example*

What Are My Thoughts In This Situation?	What Would I Think Or Say About My Best Friend Or Another Mother In This Situation?
1. The relationship with my older son will end when the baby arrives, as we will no longer have quality time together. (*all or nothing/black or white*)	1. You need to remember what a *great* relationship you have established with your older son over the years. That will not disappear when the baby is born. It is true that life will get busier when the baby arrives. However, the *quality* of time you spend with your son is just as important (if not more so) as the *quantity* of time you spend with him. It will be important to schedule times when your husband can watch the baby and you can spend an hour here or there just with your older son.
2. I should not have made the decision to have a second baby. This will be too overwhelming. (*negative filter, emotional reasoning*)	2. You and your husband love your 6-year-old very much! You both have always wanted another child as family is so important to you. Your first post-partum experience was certainly not easy and the thought of being isolated in your home or going on medication again is scary. However, you recovered soon after the postpartum period and the medication was a temporary, but necessary, solution. There are things you can do so that this postpartum phase is not the same as last time!
3. No one will be there to help me. (*probability overestimation*)	3. You started to ask for help from your mother and your sisters toward the end of your last postpartum experience and they came over much more thereafter. Although your sisters are also having babies and your mother is helping them as well, they have all voiced their sincere support and time as needed – you just have to ask!

Form 5.2 Best Friend Technique: *Juanita's Example*

What Are My Thoughts In This Situation?	What Would I Think Or Say To My Best Friend Or Another Mother In This Situation?
1.	1.
2.	2.
3.	3.

Form 5.3 Best Friend Technique

Notice in both Keesha's and Juanita's examples how self-critical and hopeless their thoughts are. However, once they were able to put some distance between the situation and themselves by imagining what they would say to their best friend, both women were able to come up with more *helpful* and *accurate* thoughts. What did you notice when completing the best friend technique with your own example?

We encourage you to practice using the best friend technique by filling out Form 5.3. You may find at first that you are best able to complete this exercise after the anxiety-provoking event has occurred (i.e., when your distress has decreased somewhat). Eventually, after practice, you will find that you can do this in the moment that you need it more automatically, without the use of paper. That is the ultimate goal. Out of the three strategies, we find the best friend technique to be the easiest 'go to' strategy to implement in the anxious moments. Women report that thinking of a loved one or another mother with compassion comes with relative ease. Although they may not believe the more balanced perspective as it applies to their own life at first, with practice, this more balanced thinking comes to feel more true over time until it is almost automatic.

Cognitive Strategy #2: Examining the Evidence

One of the most common and well-developed cognitive strategies in CBT is called 'examining the evidence.' There can often be a grain of truth to some of the negative thoughts that we experience, even though they are ultimately categorized as thinking errors. This can certainly make it more difficult to challenge unhelpful thoughts and to come up with more balanced or accurate thoughts. The goal of 'examining the evidence' is to allow us to see both sides rather than disregard the grain of truth that exists. Remember the thought from the winter weather example. Although we categorized it as a thinking error, there was truth to the thought as well – it was Monday in January and there was a blizzard. This thought becomes a thinking error when the conclusion is that 'this is going to be a horrible day so I should just stay in bed.' The example of a more balanced and helpful thought is as follows:

> While it is true that there is a blizzard outside, it is Monday morning, and it is January, it is also true that I am meeting my friend Heather for lunch and I am going to watch my nephew's basketball game in the evening. Maybe it won't be such a bad day after all.

Notice that, with this thought, the grain of truth is acknowledged *along with* the positive aspects of the day that were initially not acknowledged. The end result is a more balanced and accurate thought, packed with facts. It takes effort to come up with these facts, especially when feelings of anxiety, depression, or other negative emotions are intense, and can certainly be challenging when you are trying to do so in the moment. For this reason, you may find it more helpful to start by using this strategy when your emotions are less intense, often somewhat after the event has occurred. Similar to the 'best friend' technique, with a lot of patience and practice and by using the form provided (see Form 5.6 below), your ability to use this tool effectively in the moment will increase over time.

Try the 'examining the evidence' technique with one of the thinking errors you identified in a completed thought-monitoring form. The instructions are provided below. Use Cassandra's and Elizabeth's examples as a guide (Forms 5.4 and 5.5).

Instructions for the 'Examining the Evidence' Technique

Step 1: Using a completed thought-monitoring form, write down *one* identified thinking error.

Step 2: List all of the evidence you can find that *supports* ('evidence for') the thinking error in the first column. List all of the evidence you can find that *does not support* ('evidence against') the thinking error.

Step 3: Based on the two columns, write a revised or balanced thought at the bottom of the page.

Step 4: Reread your revised thoughts, *over and over* again, every day. These are your new balanced, more helpful, and more accurate thoughts!

Identified Thinking Error: <u>I will either have another miscarriage or something will go wrong during the labor and delivery</u> (*probability overestimation/ fortune telling*).

Evidence for My Thought

1. I miscarried during my first pregnancy and so did my sister

2. Women can miscarry well into their pregnancy

3. I had to take a couple days off from work last week, as I did not feel well

4. Emergencies can happen during labor and delivery, even with well-trained health practitioners

5.

Evidence Against My Thought

1. My healthcare team tells me every visit that my pregnancy is going well and they have no concerns

2. The further along you are in your pregnancy, the less probability of miscarrying

3. After following up with my doctor for an examination, I was medically cleared, felt well the next day, and went back to work

4. The hospital and healthcare team that is a part of your labor and delivery tell you they handle emergencies every day and point out that they have a good track record!

5.

Balanced/Accurate Thoughts

1. Even though I miscarried during my first pregnancy, my current pregnancy is going well and my healthcare team tells me they have *no concerns* at each visit.

2. Although it is still possible to miscarry, I am now in my fourth month and my doctor told me that the further along you are in your pregnancy, the less likely you are to miscarry.

3. Even though emergencies can happen in labor and delivery, I have a competent healthcare team whose members have been working in this area for a long time. They deal with emergencies every day and the hospital is equipped to handle whatever may happen. My care will be in good hands.

Form 5.4 Examining the Evidence: *Cassandra's Example*

Identified Thinking Error: <u>I am the primary caregiver and this is a lifelong job. I will never find balance again</u> (*catastrophizing/emotional reasoning*).

Evidence for My Thought	**Evidence Against My Thought**
1. I am the primary caregiver for our daughter and I am on maternity leave, so I am responsible for her care during the day	1. My husband and I both wanted to have a child and he contributes and offers to help outside of his work hours
2. The only time I see my friends is when our babies are present too – we never get together alone for coffee or lunch	2. Seeing my friends with our babies is a good first step. I can build on this
3. I only go for walks when I have the stroller. I have not gone back to the gym or started running again as I did before the baby came	3. My husband is always offering to look after the baby when he is home from work so that I can get other tasks done
4. My husband and I have not had a date night since the baby was born	4. My parents and in-laws are available to babysit for short periods of time. A couple of hours are better than nothing!
5.	5.

Balanced/Accurate Thoughts

1. Although I am the primary caregiver for our daughter with the majority of responsibility falling on my shoulders during the day, we both wanted to have a child and my husband does contribute at other times.

2. Even though there is an imbalance in my life at this time with heavy childcare responsibilities, there are things I can do to start getting more balance in my life, such as taking my husband up on his offer to look after the baby while I go for a run or see a friend for coffee.

3. Although our priorities have changed significantly since the arrival of our daughter and date nights have been non-existent, we can work to slowly change that by asking our parents to look after the baby while we spend some quality time with each other. Date nights might not be exactly the same as before but could still be enjoyable.

Form 5.5 Examining the Evidence: *Elizabeth's Example*

Examining The Evidence

Identified Thinking
Error:_____

Evidence For My Thought   **Evidence Against My Thought**

1.   1.

2.   2.

3.   3.

4.   4.

5.   5.

Balanced/Accurate Thoughts

1.

2.

3.

Form 5.6   Examining the Evidence

In both Cassandra's and Elizabeth's examples, we not only understand and appreciate why they are experiencing these thoughts but also recognize that parts of their thoughts are accurate. Upon taking some time to write down 'evidence for' and 'evidence against' their thought, Cassandra and Elizabeth developed thoughts that were both balanced and accurate. What did you notice when completing the 'examining the evidence' technique with your own examples?

Similar to the 'best friend' technique, we encourage you to practice 'examining the evidence' by writing on the form provided (Form 5.6). At first, you may find that filling in the 'Evidence For' column is easier than finding information to place in the 'Evidence Against' column. Finding facts or evidence that contradicts the negative thought often requires a great deal of effort, especially because when we feel anxious or depressed our brain is biased toward seeking out negative information (Clark & Beck, 2010; Fox et al., 2001; Franklin et al., 2005). Eventually, after practice, you will find that you can do this in the moment that you need it, without the use of paper. That is the ultimate goal.

Cognitive Strategy #3: The Possibility Pie

The next strategy is called the 'possibility pie.' A very common thinking error that we tend to make is reaching a conclusion about the outcome of a situation before it has occurred and not entertaining other possible outcomes that might be more likely (i.e., 'jumping to conclusions'). People with symptoms of anxiety and depression often predict outcomes that are negative and this tendency leads to further feelings of anxiousness and low mood. With the possibility pie technique, you can step back and consider a range of possible outcomes for a given situation and then consider how likely each of the outcomes is to be true. In the blizzard example above, the person's prediction is that 'this is going to be a horrible day.' Now that is certainly one possibility, but what are the others? What does it really mean to have a 'horrible day' anyway? Perhaps the morning will be horrible but things will get better quickly or perhaps once she gets going the day won't be so bad after all. She does have some fun plans scheduled that may lift her mood. Although you may not believe any of the alternative outcomes you generate very much at first, just the exercise of generating them can lessen the intensity of your initial thought and lead to an improvement in your mood.

Try the 'possibility pie' technique with one of the thinking errors you identified in a completed thought-monitoring form (see Form 5.9). The instructions are provided below for the use of the worksheet. Use Zoë's and Keesha's examples as a guide (Forms 5.7 and 5.8).

Instructions for the 'Possibility Pie' Technique

Step 1: Using a completed thought-monitoring form, write down *one* identified thinking error.

Step 2: Rate how much you believe that thought to be true (from 0 to 100%).

Step 3: Write down all the other possible outcomes that differ from your original thought and rate how much you believe each possible outcome to be true (0–100%).

Step 4: Re-evaluate how much you believe your original thought to be true (0–100%).

Step 5: Write down a conclusion you have come to based on the possible outcomes you have identified and your original belief.

Write down your initial thought/belief: If I let my partner help bathe the baby he won't do it properly and something bad will happen. (*probability overestimation/catastrophizing*)

Rate how much you believe the thought to be true (place your percentage in the circle)

100%

What are other possibilities? How much do you believe each to be true?

1. My partner might not wash her properly but they will enjoy their time together   (40%)

2. My partner might do a *good enough* job at bathing her but she will cry throughout   (30%)

3. My partner might do a 'good enough' job at bathing her and nothing bad will happen   (20%)

4. My partner might actually do a *great* job at bathing her and nothing bad will happen   (10%)

5. _____

Rerate your initial belief and apply it to the circle below:

50%

Conclusions: Although it is possible that my partner might not bathe the baby properly or that she will cry, it is also possible that it could go well. It is important for me to let my partner take on these tasks so he can get better at them and bond with our daughter. I need to try!

Form 5.7 Possibility Pie: *Zoë's Example*

Write down your initial thought/belief: <u>It is all my fault that my baby will not go to sleep</u> (*Probability Overestimation/Personalizing*)

Rate how much you believe the thought to be true (place your percentage in the circle)

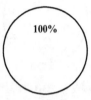

What are other possibilities? How much do you believe each to be true?

1. <u>He might be starting to teethe (irritated/sore) - he had his hand in his mouth a lot lately (30%)</u>

2. <u>He might be hungry   (25%)</u>

3. <u>He might not be tired, his morning nap went longer than it usually does   (30%)</u>

4. <u>He might be going through a growth spurt   (15%)</u>

Rerate your initial belief and apply it to the circle below:

Conclusions: <u>It is possible that do not know how to soothe my son and help get him to sleep, but it is also possible that he is teething or not yet tired, both of which are outside my control.</u>

Form 5.8 Possibility Pie: *Keesha's Example*

Write down your initial thought/belief:_____

_____

%

What are other possibilities? How much do you believe each to be true?

1._____

2._____

3._____

4._____

5._____

Rerate your initial belief and apply it to the circle below:

%

Conclusions:_____

_____

Form 5.9   Possibility Pie

Note that in Zoë's example she was able to use the possibility pie to consider a number of other possible outcomes that might occur if she allowed her husband to help bathe their baby. The additional possibilities that she was able to consider were not ones that she had first considered. However, the other possibilities (e.g., her husband might struggle somewhat at first but then learn to manage the situation over time) were potentially more realistic as outcomes and less anxiety provoking. In Keesha's case, she initially blamed herself and attributed her difficulties in getting her baby to sleep to a personal lack of skill. By the end of the exercise, she had identified a number of other likely contributors to the challenging situation and was able to develop a more balanced thought as a result. The goal is not to think unrealistically but instead to think in a more balanced and flexible way. These three tools can help women think in a more flexible way, taking into account the specific situations they find themselves in. In Table 5.1 you will find a few questions you can ask yourself to help develop a different perspective.

How Long Do I Have to Practice These Cognitive Strategies For?

What you will find as you practice these strategies is that the balanced thoughts will start to *feel* more believable and be easier to generate over time. Eventually, you will find that your brain naturally and automatically goes to a more balanced and realistic perspective and that you no longer have to make a significant effort to *think* about your thinking patterns. As you practice the strategies on a regular basis, whenever you notice that you are feeling anxious or depressed, you will find that your mood improves and your emotions are not as intense as they once were. With practice, your thinking errors, which may initially come automatically, get pushed out with alternate more balanced thoughts. Over time, your feel less anxious and depressed and you will no longer need to put in the effort of consistent practice.

So now the important question: *how long will this take?* Well, the answer is: it depends. It really depends on a few factors. We know that the more you practice, the faster this process will occur. It also depends on you and the unique aspects of your life. Each person is different and for some of you these strategies may come more naturally then others, requiring less effort. You will know when you don't have to practice regularly because you will be feeling much better and find that the situations that used to trigger anxiety or other negative feelings no longer have the same impact as you have developed new ways of approaching them. You can then dig up your practice forms and use these strategies whenever you need them in the future. We know that anxiety and depressive symptoms often fluctuate over time, particularly in times of stress. Now that you have learned these cognitive strategies, they will be there for you to rely on as a tool for managing your symptoms going forward.

Table 5.1 Questions to Challenge Thoughts

Questions to Challenge Your Anxious or Depressed Thoughts

- Have I had experiences in which my thought or prediction did *not* come true?

- What are other possible explanations for the way I'm feeling?

- What are other possible outcomes of this situation?

- Am I discounting positive experiences and focusing on my fears?

- Are there any strengths in me that I am ignoring?

- What would I say to a friend or a loved one if he or she was having these thoughts?

- If my feared prediction came true, how bad would that really be?

- If I feel embarrassed, how long will this embarrassment last? Will they definitely think negative things?

- I may feel uncomfortable, but is that a *horrible* or *unbearable* outcome?

- Even if my thought is true (e.g., 'I am so upset/angry right now'), how helpful is it to think this thought over and over? Is it adding to or taking away from my distress?

Activity for Practice

Over the next week, continue using the thought-monitoring form from Chapter 4. With the thinking errors you identified within your forms, try each of the three cognitive strategies at least once. It will be helpful to set aside some time each day to work on this homework.

Summing It All Up

Thoughts that contain thinking errors are generally thoughts that are unhelpful and do not take the full situation into account. These thoughts are likely adding to your distress and need to be challenged. The goal in challenging unhelpful thoughts is not to simply replace them with unrealistically positive thoughts but instead to develop thoughts that are more balanced – that take both the challenging *and* more positive aspects of a situation into account. The more balanced our thoughts are, the less likely we are to experience intense anxiety or depression on an ongoing basis. The three cognitive strategies presented in this chapter, the 'best friend' technique, the 'examining the evidence' technique, and the 'possibility pie,' can be used to challenge a thought that contains thinking errors and to help guide you as you work at generating more balanced, helpful, and more accurate thoughts in the situations that make you anxious. Although this process can take time and effort at first, it is well worth the effort. The more you practice using these techniques, the better able you will be to think in a more balanced and helpful way. Over time, with practice, you will find that your distress decreases with less effort.

References

Clark, D. A., & Beck, T. A. (2010). Cognitive theory and therapy of anxiety and depression: Convergence with neurobiological findings. *Trends in Cognitive Sciences, 14*, 418–424. doi:10.1016/j.tics.2010.06.007

Fox, E., Russo, R., & Dutton, K. (2001). Attentional bias for threat: Evidence for delayed disengagement from emotional faces. *Cognition and Emotion, 16*, 355–379. doi:10.1080/02699930143000527

Franklin, M. E., Huppert, J., Langner, R., Leiberg, S., & Foa, E. B. (2005). Interpretation bias: A comparison of treated social phobics, untreated social phobics, and controls. *Cognitive Therapy and Research, 29*, 289–300. doi:10.1007/s10608-005-2412-8

Chapter 6

Problem Solving with Productive Worry

What Is the Difference between Productive and Unproductive Worry?
How Should I Handle Unproductive Worry?
What Should I Do When My Worry is Productive?

Arriving at this chapter means that you have gained more awareness of what influences your anxiety, depression, and other negative feelings through use of the thought-monitoring form in Chapter 4. As you recall, this tool is the first step in the cognitive behavioral therapy (CBT) approach. It allows you to break down your anxious or depressed experiences in part by helping you to identify the thoughts that are contributing to your distress, and more specifically, any *thinking errors*.

In Chapter 5, you learned how to change your thoughts that contain thinking errors into more accurate, balanced thoughts with the use of three cognitive strategies: the 'best friend' technique, 'examining the evidence' technique, and the 'possibility pie' technique. Even though we will be introducing new content and another strategy in this chapter, these three cognitive strategies need to be practiced on a regular basis, so that they start making an ongoing difference in how you feel. Practicing these strategies, especially at the start of this program, is the key to *retraining your brain*. We want your brain to start 'choosing' to turn to the new accurate thoughts you developed with these strategies instead of turning back to the old thinking errors.

For instance, after Cassandra completed her 'examining the evidence' worksheet and developed more accurate thoughts including, 'Even though I miscarried during my first pregnancy, my current pregnancy is going well and my healthcare team tells me they have no concerns at each visit' and 'Although it is still possible to miscarry, I am now in my fourth month and my doctor told me that the further along you are in your pregnancy, the less likely you are to miscarry,' she found that she had to remind herself of these more balanced thoughts throughout the day. She even wrote the more helpful thoughts on a cue card that she carried in her purse so that she could reread them before attending future doctor's appointments.

When people are first learning to develop balanced thoughts they often say that they know the balanced statement is true at a *cognitive* (rational) level but they don't 'feel' it is true at an *emotional* level. To get to that emotional level, you will need to practice and remind yourself of the balanced thought regularly as your mind will more naturally generate the view that leads to feeling more anxious or depressed for some time. Through ongoing practice, you will find that the balanced thought starts to 'feel' more believable.

Another step to challenging your worry thoughts is to really identify what it is you fear will happen. The first step in this process is changing the format of your worry thought from a question to a statement.

Transforming Worry Questions to Worry Statements

Worry thoughts can be defined as thoughts about the future with a focus on a negative or unfavorable outcome. Everyone worries from time to time and pregnancy and the postpartum period can be particularly difficult times for women, especially those who already tend to worry quite a bit. As we have discussed, there is an endless list of possible worries for mothers and mothers-to-be. These worries are sometimes expressed as a question, often starting with '*what if . . .*' Underlying the '*what if . . .*' question is usually a specific feared consequence that you may or may not be consciously aware of. The first step in uncovering what you are worried about is to reframe your question as a statement of what it is you are *actually worried* will happen (see examples in Table 6.1). Reframing the *worry question* into a *worry statement* will then allow you to use the cognitive strategies you have already learned in Chapter 5 as well as the new problem-solving strategy you will learn in this chapter.

Once you have reframed your statement it should be quite clear why it is leading you to feel anxious or depressed. If it is unclear and ambiguous, you should add a bit more detail. For example, Juanita had the worry 'Will I have help when I need it?' and reframed it to the statement 'I will not have help when I need it'. However, the statement still needs more detail as it is not clear why not having help would lead her to feel anxious. She thought a bit more about what she was really afraid would happen and then added more to the thought to reveal her core fear: 'I will not have help when I need it and I will develop postpartum depression again.' When you are practicing reframing worry questions to worry statements, we encourage you to dig deep and discover what is really at the root of your worry in a way that is very specific and detailed. The more specific and detailed your worry statement is, the easier it will be for you to challenge it and generate a more balanced thought.

As mentioned in the previous chapters, we do not expect every thought that is written down on your thought-monitoring form to contain a thinking error. You may have already noticed this as you are evaluating your thoughts in the 'Thoughts' column over the past couple of weeks. You may have further noticed

Table 6.1 Worry Questions to Worry Statements

	Worry Question	*Worry Statement*
Cassandra	Will I have a baby that is healthy?	There will be health problems when my baby is born
Juanita	Will I have help when I need it?	I will not have help when I need it and I will develop postpartum depression again
Zoë	What if I am not a good mom?	I will make mistakes while trying to take care of my baby and will not be a good mom
Keesha	Will other people think I am incompetent as a parent?	Other people will think I am incompetent with my parenting if my baby cries and I can't soothe him
Elizabeth	There has been no time for each other – will my marriage end in divorce?	My marriage could end in divorce if there is no time for each other because of the new baby

that some of the thoughts that are contributing to your anxiety and depression are *accurate* worries. These thoughts are called *productive worries*. Productive worries do *not* contain thinking errors and require an action-oriented strategy. Read on to learn more about what productive worries are and how to distinguish between a productive worry and an unproductive worry (also known as a thinking error).

What Is Productive Worry Versus Unproductive Worry?

Worry is considered helpful when the worry directs your attention to a problem that needs to be solved and leads you to take action. For instance, *worrying* that you need to find good childcare prior to your return to work may push you to research your options and make a decision well before you go back. Worry is considered unhelpful when it is excessive or unmanageable, interferes with your life and in your relationships, and/or causes other problems such as procrastination in addition to anxiety and depression.

As outlined in Figure 6.1, there are two types of worry: *productive worry* and *unproductive worry*. Learning how to determine whether your worry is productive or unproductive is the first step. Once you are able to categorize a worry thought as either productive or unproductive, you will be able to decide which strategies will be most helpful going forward.

The exercise in Table 6.2 allows you to practice categorizing a worry thought as productive or unproductive. For each of the following worry thoughts, determine

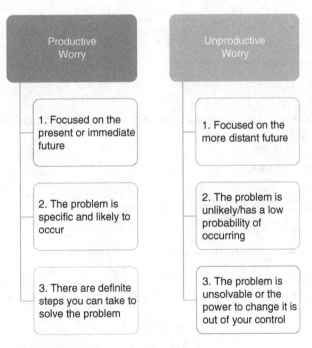

Figure 6.1 Productive Versus Unproductive Worry

Table 6.2 Productive Versus Unproductive Worry Exercise

1. I had sushi once before I knew I was pregnant – this will cause my baby to have a birth defect (*Cassandra*)

   Productive or unproductive?_____

   Why?_____

   _____

2. I need to get childcare before I return to work – I worry I won't find any (*Elizabeth*)

   Productive or unproductive?_____

   Why?_____

   _____

3. I worry I will find childcare but it will turn out that I don't like the organization (*Elizabeth*)

   Productive or unproductive?_____

   Why?_____

   _____

4. I worry I will not get the help and support I need and I will develop postpartum depression again (*Juanita*)

   Productive or unproductive?_____

   Why?_____

   _____

5. I worry I have made the wrong decision to leave my baby alone with my partner while I go to my doctor's appointment (*Zoë*)

   Productive or unproductive?_____

   Why?_____

whether it is a productive or unproductive worry based on the criteria in Figure 6.1. Give at least one reason for your answer.

Answers: Productive versus Unproductive Worry Exercise

Cassandra's worry is *unproductive* because it has a low likelihood of occurring. For instance, the chance that eating uncooked food on one evening prior to realizing she was pregnant will have caused harm to her infant is extremely low. Further, it is an unproductive worry because the power to change this situation is out of her control. Cassandra cannot go back in time and *not* eat sushi on that evening so there is no action for her to take at this time.

Elizabeth's first worry is *productive* because it is specific and is highly likely to occur. She will be returning to work and will need to find childcare for her daughter. It is also *productive* because there are definite steps she can take to solve the problem. However, Elizabeth's second worry is *unproductive*. She wants her childcare to be perfect for her daughter. She worries that even if she does find childcare, she might not like the organization. In this case, the worry is *unproductive* since it is in the more distant future (she needs to actually find childcare first). Further, the problem has a low likelihood of occurring since she knows that she would not sign her daughter up for a childcare that does not meet her needs/standards. If, down the road, Elizabeth chooses a childcare that *does not* turn out to be a good fit, this same worry would become a productive worry and would warrant problem solving, but just not now!

Juanita's worry is a *productive* worry because it has a high likelihood of occurring. Specifically, since Juanita developed postpartum depression after the birth of her first baby, she is at increased risk for developing it again. Further, since she has not yet gathered the help and support from her family and friends that she will need in the postpartum, there is a higher likelihood that her depressive symptoms could recur. Finally, this is a *productive* worry because Juanita has the power to take steps that could change this situation by taking a problem-solving approach.

Zoë's worry is *unproductive* because the power to change it is out of her control (she is now at the doctor's appointment) and the likelihood that the decision was wrong and that something bad will happen is very low. Her partner has looked after the baby in the past and has done just fine so there is no prior evidence to support her worry.

Problem Solving with Productive Worries

If you have analyzed a worry thought and determined that it is an *unproductive worry* (also known as a thinking error) using the criteria in Figure 6.1, you can use one of the three cognitive strategies to challenge this worry and come up with a more accurate thought. However, if you analyzed a worry thought and determined that it is a *productive worry*, you will use a different approach, namely, the *problem-solving* strategy to identify effective solutions to address the issue that is generating the worry. The following *problem-solving* strategy uses an action-oriented approach to work with your worry. Remember, a *productive worry* means that the worry is:

1. realistic and likely to happen

2. based in the present or in the near future

3. something that you could control or solve if you tried.

Use Elizabeth's and Keesha's examples as a guide (Forms 6.1 and 6.2).

Instructions: Problem-Solving Strategy

Step 1: Define the problem, being as specific as possible. Define your goal, being sure to write what you would like to be different (e.g., how would it look?).

Step 2: Generate possible solutions. Write down every possible solution you can imagine, no matter how silly they may seem.

Step 3: Choose the best solution. Pick the solution that you think has the best chance of success and seems most workable.

Step 4: Break down the solution into smaller steps that would be needed to achieve the goal.

Step 5: Decide on a time to start. Begin!

1. **Define the problem and goal.**

   Problem: I will be returning to work following maternity leave and I do not have childcare.

   Goal: I need to find childcare well in advance.

2. **Generate possible solutions.**

   - Start asking friends
   - Look into organized daycare in my city
   - Look into private home-based daycare options
   - Work part-time and obtain part-time care from Grandma
   - Change work – find work that I can do from home

3. **Choose the best solution.**

   Look into organized daycare in my city

4. **Break the solution down into manageable steps.**

   (a) Write out what my needs are in a daycare/what I will and will not compromise on
   (b) Start asking friends where they go (and how they made their decision)
   (c) Start a thorough search on the internet/pick up pamphlets from resource centers
   (d) Start contacting daycares in my area that appear to meet my needs for a visit
   (e) Make a short list of daycares I like and allow time to make a decision

5. **Decide on a time to begin.**

   On the weekend when my husband is home and the baby is napping in the afternoon, I will start by writing out my needs and searching the internet.

Form 6.1 Problem-Solving Strategy: Elizabeth's Example

Notice that many of the possible solutions that Elizabeth generated are reasonable and feasible. Choosing the best solution from her list of possible solutions required her to consider what would work best for her, for her family, and her life circumstances. She decided she would prefer an organized childcare setting. If she pursues this option and decides later that it is not going to work she can always return to her list of possible solutions and pick a different option.

Elizabeth is very specific in the steps that she will take to implement her solution. This level of detail is very helpful as it breaks down the steps so that the whole process is less overwhelming. Elizabeth had felt like this issue had been hanging over her head and making her miserable. Once she completed this form, she felt less overwhelmed and better able to take the steps she needed to solve her childcare problem.

1. Define the problem and goal.

Problem: My second baby is arriving soon and I have not arranged for any help when I get home with the baby.

Goal: I need to arrange for people to help with the baby and household so that I can take better care of myself (and reduce the risk of another period of postpartum depression), while also giving me the chance to have quality time with my older son.

2. Generate possible solutions.

- Call my mother and discuss times when she can commit to coming each week
- Call my sisters to arrange regular visits with our children in the first 3 months
- Look into babysitting services I noticed at our community center
- Ask if my in-laws could take my older son on afternoons when I am running errands
- See if neighbour's 14-year-old daughter would like to earn money and help around the house while I am at home with the children

3. Choose the best solution.

Call my mother and discuss times when she can commit to coming each week

4. Break the solution down into manageable steps.

(a) Reflect on what would be most helpful for me (e.g., time of day, day of the week)
(b) Write down the activities that would be important to receive help with (e. g., laundry)
(c) Contact my mother to arrange a time to discuss this
(d) Speak to my mother about my needs, and work together with her schedule to arrange consistent help

5. Decide on a time to begin.

Call her on Wednesday and ask if she can come over to discuss this on Thursday

Form 6.2 Problem-Solving Strategy: Juanita's Example

Like Elizabeth, Juanita had also generated a number of reasonable solutions. In the end, she felt that starting with getting help from her mother was the best choice based on her comfort level and preferences. Depending on what her mother is able to commit to, Juanita may need to add others who can also help with childcare so that she has as much support as she needs. Juanita was very specific in listing the steps she needs to take to carry out her preferred solution, including really thinking about what her specific needs were and the best timing. She can then use this information to guide the conversation with her mother. If things don't go as planned, she can then return to her list of possible solutions to select another option.

Now think of a worry that you have that would be considered a productive worry. You may find it helpful to return to the thought-monitoring forms you have completed and look in the 'Thoughts' column. You may need to change the worry from a question to a statement, as illustrated at the beginning of this chapter. Once it is in a statement form, you will likely find that you have identified a clear problem that is in need of a solution. Use the problem-solving strategy in Form 6.3 to develop an action plan for addressing this problem.

1. Define the problem and goal.

_____

_____

_____

_____

2. Generate possible solutions.

- _____

- _____

- _____

- _____

- _____

3. Choose the best solution.

_____

4. Break the solution down into manageable steps.

a._____

b._____

c._____

d._____

e._____

5. Decide on a time to begin.

_____

Form 6.3 Problem-Solving Strategy

Activity for Practice

Over the next week, continue using the thought-monitoring form from Chapter 4 and the three cognitive strategies from Chapter 5. In addition, try to use the problem-solving strategy at least once with a productive worry. It will be helpful to set aside some time each day to work on this homework.

Summing It All Up

In this chapter, you learned how to identify two types of worry: productive and unproductive. Unproductive worry is associated with anxiety and generally contains thinking errors (e.g., catastrophic or worst-case scenario thinking). When worries contain thinking errors, these thoughts need to be challenged and changed into more balanced or more helpful thoughts using one of the three cognitive strategies you learned in Chapter 5 (i.e., the 'best friend' technique, the 'evidence technique', or the 'possibility pie' technique).

However, *productive* worries do not contain thinking errors and are instead an accurate reflection of an anxiety-provoking situation. These worries are productive if they are: (1) about a situation that is current or will occur in the near future; (2) about a situation that you can do something about; and (3) about a situation where the negative outcome has a higher likelihood of occurring if action is not taken.

When worries are productive, an action-oriented or problem-solving strategy is needed. This strategy is particularly helpful when feeling overwhelmed or when anxiety or depression is getting in the way of your usual problem-solving strategies. An effective problem-solving approach begins with identifying a clear, specific problem and goal in solving the problem. Next, a list of possible solutions is generated. Finally, the solution that seems most likely to meet your goal(s) and solve the problem is chosen. If your solution did not solve the problem, you may find that you have new knowledge about the problem that helps guide you to another, more effective solution.

Chapter 7

Addressing Problematic Behaviors Using Therapeutic Exposure

What Are Problematic Behaviors and How Do I Identify Them?

What is Therapeutic Exposure?

How Long Do I Have to Practice Therapeutic Exposure?

So far, you have worked on the 'C' in cognitive behavioral therapy (CBT). Chapters 4 through 6 helped you to recognize how powerful thoughts are in contributing to anxiety, depression, and other negative emotions. By learning to use strategies such as the 'best friend' technique, 'examining the evidence,' and the 'possibility pie,' you can take your identified thinking errors and change them into more balanced and accurate thoughts. With practice, these new balanced thoughts can reduce anxiety and depression and have a positive influence on how you feel. Using the thought-monitoring form (Chapter 4), you have also learned that *not all* of your thoughts are thinking errors. Instead, some of the worries you have are *productive worries* and require a practical problem-solving strategy to reduce your distress. Remember how much better Juanita felt after she applied the problem-solving strategy to her productive worry 'I won't have the help I need when my baby is born' (Chapter 6). Using the problem-solving strategy, she was able to come up with a step-by-step approach to resolving her worry. She reached out for help and put support in place to reduce her anxiety.

The fact is, thoughts are powerful and have a tremendous impact on how we feel. It is also true that thoughts have a tremendous impact on our behavior. Refer to the cognitive behavioral model in Figure 7.1.

Recall the cold-weather example from Chapter 4 and the thought, 'It is Monday, the middle of January, and there is a blizzard outside. This is going to be a horrible day; I might as well stay in bed.' This thought, if not changed to a more balanced or accurate thought, may influence the person's behavior, causing her to stay in bed instead of getting up. Now, in addition to a thinking error ('this is going to be a horrible day') we also have a *problematic behavior* – staying in bed! Problematic behaviors, like the

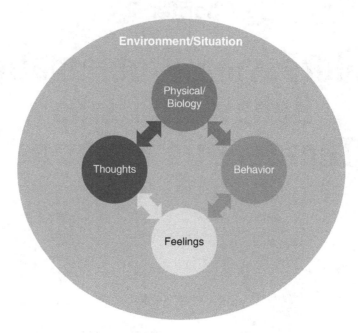

Figure 7.1 The Cognitive Behavioral Model

one in the example above, can seem like a good idea when we first engage in them because they tend to give us relief and reduce our anxiety and depression, at least initially. However, in the long run they can produce more distress and impairment.

Similar to common categories of thinking errors, there are common categories of problematic behaviors that are observed in individuals with anxiety and depression. These categories (described in the next section) include avoidance and escape, reassurance seeking, and checking and repeating (Abramowitz & Moore, 2007; Beesdo-Baum et al., 2012; Salkovskis, 1991). In this chapter, each of these behaviors will be discussed in detail. You will learn a powerful strategy to reduce problematic behaviors – *therapeutic exposure*. The problematic behavior that is most common in individuals with depression is withdrawal from activity and social isolation. This will be the focus of Chapter 8. Below is a list of common ways people react to anxiety in terms of their behavioral responses.

Common Types of Problematic Coping Behaviors

Avoidance and Escape

The most common type of problematic behavior in response to anxiety is *avoidance*. The general belief driving avoidance is that if you stay away from your fears, these fears will not come true. There is also the belief that you will be safer if you stay put and do not follow through with a situation or task. This works effectively in the short term to reduce your anxiety; however, in the long term it can significantly limit your life.

Consider an example from Keesha: she is fearful that if she goes to the grocery store her baby will start crying uncontrollably and others will judge her. Keesha decides to take her coat off, put her diaper bag away, and stay home. She asks her husband to pick up pizza on his way home from work for the third time this week. Keesha feels immediate relief and her anxiety decreases once she has chosen not to leave her house. In the long term, however, avoidance may decrease her self-esteem, reduce her confidence in her ability to cope, and will cause Keesha to rely on others more and more. Avoidance will also make it difficult for Keesha to tackle the same situation next time it comes up and can lead to a worsening of her anxiety such that it becomes a vicious cycle.

Similarly, when you feel anxious, the urge to *escape* a situation that you perceive to be dangerous makes sense biologically. It is a protective response in the face of real danger. But when no danger is present, choosing to escape can be counterproductive, especially over time. While escaping a situation can be very effective for reducing your anxiety in the short term, in the long run you are allowing your anxiety to take control of your life. The more situations that you avoid and escape, the greater the impact anxiety has on your ability to function and your quality of life. Anxiety is making the decisions in your life and calling the shots, not you. This way, your self-confidence will significantly decrease over time, which will help perpetuate this vicious cycle.

Examples: Avoidance and Escape

Keesha's Example

Keesha has avoided going out with her baby as well as having family and friends over to her home. Her anxious prediction is that others will negatively judge her ability to care for her baby and the choices she has made for her son. Further, if she does make it to places such as the grocery store and her baby starts to cry, she will escape these situations since she believes that they will never end or will be intolerable.

Pros of Avoidance/Escape: By avoiding having her family and friends over, Keesha does not have to endure the visit. By escaping from places like the grocery store, she experiences an immediate relief from anxiety.

Cons of Avoidance/Escape: By not having her family and friends over, she does not get to visit with them, and they do not get to see the baby and form a relationship with him. In addition, the relationship with her husband, who would like to have his family over, is becoming strained. By escaping from the grocery store, Keesha does not get the groceries she needs for dinner and her husband is taxed with picking up pizza again, which is getting to be costly. She also feels frustrated with herself and starts to feel like her identity of a confident, calm person is now changing. She wonders if she will ever feel *normal* again.

Zoë's Example

Zoë has avoided having her partner bathe the baby in the infant tub. Her anxious prediction is that something bad will happen, that he will make mistakes, and the baby will be upset and will cry uncontrollably.

Pros of Avoidance/Escape: By not letting her partner bathe the baby, Zoë gets to stay in control and can continually monitor the safety and well-being of her baby.

Cons of Avoidance/Escape: By not letting her partner bathe the baby, Zoë is preventing him from learning how to take care of the baby, which in turn may prevent him from becoming more confident as a parent and enjoying a new bonding activity with his daughter. Further, Zoë is losing the opportunity of a much-needed break from childcare, leading to increased fatigue and a continued lack of balance in her life. Finally, when Zoë is tired, she tends to worry more. So in the end she has an increase in overall anxiety.

Can you think of any situations or tasks that you tend to avoid or escape due to anxiety? List the situations or tasks that you avoid in Form 7.1. Now consider the pros of avoidance/escape. What motivates your avoidance/escape? How does avoidance/escape help you? Now consider the cons of avoidance/escape. How does your avoidance/escape negatively impact your life and relationships?

Situations I Avoid/Escape

_____

_____

_____

Pros of Avoidance/Escape: _____

_____

_____

Cons of Avoidance/Escape: _____

_____

_____

Form 7.1 Situations I Avoid/Escape

Reassurance Seeking

We all need to seek reassurance from time to time. Doing so can reduce worry and increase our sense that we will be able to cope. Excessive reassurance seeking, however, is another common form of problematic behavior in response to anxiety. Babies do not come with instruction manuals and even if they did, each one is unique. Parenting is one of the most important roles of your life and we can appreciate that you do not want to make mistakes. An increased tendency to seek reassurance as a mother-to-be or new mother is understandable during this time. You might ask for reassurance from family, friends, or health professionals. You might find yourself checking the internet for information to reduce your anxiety.

The essence of *excessive* reassurance seeking, however, is the attempt to eliminate *all* doubt and make *absolutely certain* you are on the right track, even in situations where it is not possible to be 100% certain. Because this degree of certainty is virtually impossible to achieve, individuals who frequently worry or feel anxious often find themselves seeking reassurance again and again, without the desired reduction in their worry or anxiety. If this is the case for you, excessive reassurance seeking has likely become a problematic behavior and may be interfering in your day-to-day life. Similarly to repeated avoidance, the use of repeated or excessive reassurance seeking can undermine a person's confidence in her ability to cope and may actually *maintain* anxiety.

Examples: Reassurance Seeking

Cassandra's Example

Cassandra seeks excessive reassurance from her family doctor and her obstetrician, asking if the baby is OK multiple times within an appointment and requesting more medical tests to make sure everything is all right. Cassandra also searches the internet to make sure she or her medical team is not missing anything. Her anxious prediction is that if she does not seek reassurance in this excessive way something bad will happen because something important will have been missed.

Pros of Reassurance Seeking: She gets to hear that everything is OK from her medical team and this reduces her anxiety in the moment.

Cons of Reassurance Seeking: She continues to worry again shortly after she leaves. The uncertainty continues. She notices that the relief she feels after hearing the reassurance from others is only short-lived.

Juanita's Example

Juanita seeks reassurance from her husband about whether they made the right decision to have a second baby. She will call him several times at work to ask if he still thinks a second baby is the right decision and this continues to be a topic of conversation when he gets home. If he does not answer her texts right away or if he is abrupt in his responses to her when discussing this at home, Juanita fears that it means that he is having second thoughts and that this decision was a mistake.

Pros of Reassurance Seeking: Juanita's anxiety decreases for the moment when she hears her husband providing reassurance that he wants the baby and that they made the right decision.

Cons of Reassurance Seeking: Her reliance on her husband to reassure her is straining their relationship. It also does not allow Juanita to rely on herself and build her own confidence in her decision making. Further, seeking reassurance is a short-term fix because her anxiety usually returns, at times only minutes later.

Are there times when you engage in excessive reassurance seeking? Describe ways that you seek reassurance in Form 7.2. Then consider the advantages of your reassurance-seeking behavior. What motivates you to seek reassurance? Now consider the disadvantages of seeking reassurance. How might it have a negative impact on your life? How does it affect your confidence and your relationships?

Situations In Which I Seek Reassurance

_____

_____

_____

Pros of Seeking Reassurance:_____

_____

_____

Cons of Seeking Reassurance_____

_____

_____

Form 7.2 Situations In Which I Seek Reassurance

Checking and Repeating

Checking and repeating behaviors are most often motivated by a specific fear or worry and the need to feel in control and prevent bad things from happening. For example, you may fear that your baby will get sick and so you repeatedly wash his bottles and soothers to feel sure they are clean enough for him to use. We all check or repeat a behavior from time to time and, when not in excess, checking and repeating are OK. However, these behaviors become problematic when they start to be time consuming, interfere with your life, or cause problems in your relationships. These behaviors may lessen your anxiety in the short term, directly after you check or repeat, but your anxiety quickly flares up again, motivating further checking and repeating behavior.

Examples: Checking and Repeating

Zoë's Example

Zoë checks the baby throughout the night to see if she is still breathing. She fears that if she does not get up and check several times the baby might stop breathing and she will not notice and be unable to help.

Pros of Checking/Repeating: Zoë feels relief and reduced anxiety each time she checks her baby and sees that she is breathing. She feels that she is in control and preventing a potential catastrophic outcome.

Cons of Checking/Repeating: Zoë does not get the sleep that she needs as a result of checking multiple times during the night and is even more exhausted the next day. Because of this, Zoë cannot get everything done that she planned to do the next day. Due to exhaustion, she feels more anxious and upset. As a result, she becomes more irritable with her family. Finally, Zoë does not give herself the opportunity to test whether repeated checking over the night is really necessary.

Elizabeth's Example

Elizabeth admits that she has high standards for herself in her role as a mother. She tends to check things and pay attention to detail with several tasks throughout the day to make sure that she has done them correctly and, strives to do these tasks 'perfectly.' These tasks can include folding and doing laundry for her baby and cleaning her room to preparing her bottles. Elizabeth believes that if she does not do this – if the tasks she completes are not done 'perfectly' – she will be failing in her role as a mother. She will often redo a task repeatedly until she feels it meets her standards.

Pros of Checking/Repeating: Elizabeth feels satisfied when she takes extra time and checks that tasks are done to her standards. She notices a reduction in her anxiety in the short term. She feels more in control when everything around her is in line with her high standards.

Cons of Checking/Repeating: <u>Because of all the time it takes to complete and repeat her tasks until they meet her high standards, Elizabeth falls behind on other chores and errands and stays up later at night to get them done, sacrificing sleep and increasing fatigue. She often feels overwhelmed by the disorder around her and her inability to achieve what she wants in the day. Further, Elizabeth is not 'present' or in the moment when she is playing with her daughter, since she is always thinking about whether she completed a previous task perfectly and what she needs to tackle next.</u>

Are there times when you are checking or repeating a behavior as a way of reducing your anxiety and feeling more in control? Take some time to list these behaviors in Form 7.3. Then consider the pros of your checking/repeating behavior. What motivates you to engage in checking/repeating behavior? What are the cons of these behaviors? How do they negatively impact your life?

Situations In Which I Engage in Checking or Repeating

_____

_____

_____

Pros of Checking/Repeating:_____

_____

_____

Cons of Checking/Repeating:_____

_____

_____

Form 7.3 Situations In Which I Engage in Checking or Repeating

Reducing Problematic Behaviors Using Therapeutic Exposure

Exposure to feared situations in a gradual manner is a highly effective strategy for reducing and eliminating the problematic behaviors we have covered in this chapter, including avoidance/escape, reassurance seeking, and checking/repeating behaviors. By gradually putting yourself in the situations you fear without checking, repeating, or seeking reassurance, your anxiety decreases and your confidence increases. Exposure retrains your brain as it provides an opportunity for you to learn that your feared predictions do not come true. We call it *therapeutic* exposure as you are purposely engaging in the exposure in a planned way to reduce anxiety. This is in contrast to everyday exposure where you may be put in one of your feared situations and respond in an anxious manner by using one of the problematic behaviors described above.

Treating a Fear of Dogs Using Therapeutic Exposure

Sometimes it can be helpful to understand a concept or how a strategy works if we put a little distance between the concept and our own experiences. The following example using a fear of dogs is offered for this purpose. It focuses on something very different but the commonality is treating *anxiety* using therapeutic exposure.

Imagine you are a psychologist who specializes in the treatment of anxiety. You have an appointment for the first time with a man named John who says he wants treatment for his fear of dogs (also known as a dog phobia). You ask John why he fears dogs and he replies:

> I was bitten by a dog when I was young. I fear that if I go near a dog, I will be bitten again, will need to go to the hospital, and will end up with horrendous injuries and hideous permanent scars.

John starts to tell you how his life is affected by his fear of dogs. He mentions that there are small ways in which his fear affects his daily life, such as crossing the street to walk on the other side if he sees a dog coming toward him. John reveals other ways his fear of dogs impacts his life, including avoiding parks or hiking trails. He enjoys picnics and hiking and so this is upsetting to him as he is no longer able to engage in these activities. However, the biggest area of impact in John's life, and for which he is seeking treatment, is that he avoids going to his new in-laws' home because they have a golden retriever. This has placed a significant strain on the relationship John has not only with his in-laws but with his new wife as well.

Although you can appreciate why John is anxious about dogs and can understand why he avoids them, you can probably also identify the thinking errors in John's thoughts. Specifically, John is engaging in *probability overestimation* since he is overestimating the likelihood that, if he encounters a dog, it will bite him. He is also engaged in *catastrophizing* since his prediction is much more severe than the result of the dog bite he had when he was younger (minor scar on his calf). He is predicting that the worst-case scenario will occur and he will 'end up with horrendous injuries and hideous permanent scars.'

You are already well versed in what to do when you identify a thinking error, so you decide to teach John the three cognitive strategies you have learned, including the best friend technique, examining the evidence, and the possibility pie, to help him develop a more balanced and accurate way of thinking. However, despite using these strategies to challenge his anxious thoughts, John continues to engage in extensive *avoidance*. The consequences of his avoidance are significant. He is not able to fully enjoy his life and his relationships with his in-laws and wife are strained. John also never has the opportunity to see if his feared prediction comes true.

What should John's therapeutic exposure treatment look like and what should he tackle first? The recommended way to go about exposure is to do so by *gradually* engaging in the avoided situations. So, instead of taking John to the police station to be around well-trained German shepherd police dogs, we may want to start with having him walk to a fenced in park where dogs play. Clearly the former situation would cause more anxiety than the latter! Making a list of situations from most anxiety to least anxiety, also known as a *hierarchy of feared situations*, is important as it will help you determine where to start with your therapeutic exposures.

Hierarchy of Feared Situations and the Habituation Curve

The first step in creating a hierarchy of feared situations is to make a list of the situations you are avoiding, seeking reassurance for, or checking/repeating because of your anxiety. Next, rate how anxious you would be in each of these situations using a rating scale from 0 ('not at all anxious') to 100 ('extremely anxious'). The next step is to organize the list starting with the most anxiety-provoking situation at the top and ending with the least anxiety-provoking situation at the bottom so that your fears are ranked from highest to lowest. Below are Zoë's (Table 7.1) and Keesha's (Table 7.2) hierarchies as examples.

Once you have completed your hierarchy, you can begin practicing the situations that are difficult for you. You can be as gradual in your approach to confronting the situations that cause you anxiety as you need to be so that it is not overwhelming for you. You will typically start with situations that are lower on your hierarchy first, such as a situation in which your anxiety would be 40–50. This range is considered *challenging but manageable*.

The goal is to practice entering into the selected situation on your hierarchy repeatedly (multiple times a day or once a day over several days depending on the situation) until you find your anxiety associated with the situation begin to decrease, also known as the *habituation curve* (Figure 7.2).

Table 7.1 Hierarchy of Feared Situations: *Zoë's Example*	
Situations	*Anxiety Level (0–100)*
Sleep through the night, only waking up to check on the baby if needed (e.g., if she cries, needs to feed)	90
Reduce my checking to make sure the baby is breathing in the night by half (once every 2 hours instead of once an hour)	60
Have my partner bathe the baby in the infant tub (while I am out of the room)	55
Have my partner bathe the baby in the infant tub (while I am watching)	45
Wash the baby myself but have my partner dry her after the bath and put lotion and pajamas on her	25

Table 7.2 Hierarchy of Feared Situations: *Keesha's Example*	
Situations	*Anxiety Level (0–100)*
Go to grocery store with baby and stay even if the baby is crying	100
Go to grocery store with baby and husband	75
Have my in-laws over for a visit	65
Have my girlfriends over for a visit	50
Attend a library story time class with my baby	40
Go for a walk in the neighborhood with the stroller	30

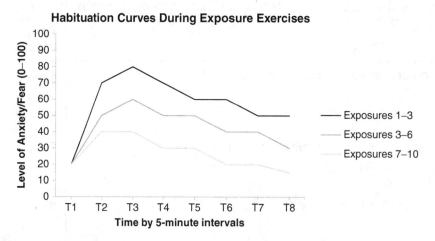

Figure 7.2 Habituation Curve

Again, you will repeatedly practice the situation until your anxiety is reduced and then move up to the next level. As you practice each situation, you will gain confidence. You will also probably find that the items at the top of your hierarchy no longer provoke the same level of anxiety as they initially did so that, when you finally get to them, they seem more manageable. Once your anxiety has decreased in a specific situation, you can move up the hierarchy to try the next most anxiety-provoking situation on your list. Below are Zoë's and Keesha's plans as an example.

Zoë's Plan

This week I will focus on bath time. I will ask my partner to take over bathing the baby and stand back without interfering. I will practice this a few times and then I will practice not being in the bathroom during bath time.

For Zoë's plan, she has decided to start with the bath time routine as she feels that starting higher up in her hierarchy (e.g., not checking her baby during the night) would be too overwhelming at first. She finds the situation of not doing the bath time herself anxiety provoking, at a score of 45, but manageable. She found after two times watching her partner bathe the baby with her present that her anxiety decreased (down to 20) and she moved up the hierarchy to having her partner bathe the baby without her present. After three practices her anxiety decreased from 55 to 20 (Form 7.4). She and her partner agreed to a plan going forward where they would take turns bathing the baby. It is very important to continue to practice the situations on your hierarchy even after your anxiety is reduced to maintain the gains that you achieve and prevent a return of fear.

Over the course of a few weeks, while she was practicing not checking on the baby at night, Zoë was able to get some good sleep and her anxiety was greatly reduced. She used the cognitive strategies she learned, especially the possibility pie and best friend techniques, to manage her urges to check the baby in the night. She would like to work towards only checking the baby when she knows the baby needs her (e.g., when the baby is crying or hungry).

Keesha's Plan

I will go for a walk in the neighborhood with my baby in the stroller and plan to do this twice a day – in the morning and afternoon. When this is easier I will try attending a story time class at the library with my baby.

Keesha started with the first item on her hierarchy. It was a good idea for her to plan two walks a day as we know that the more you practice a situation, the easier it gets and the faster your anxiety decreases. After 3 days of twice-daily walks with her baby, Keesha rated her anxiety as a 10. Initially, she found using the cognitive strategies during the walk helpful to tackle the thoughts that would pop up (e.g., that people were noticing her and judging her), especially when her baby was crying. On the fourth day, she noticed that she was paying more attention to things around her on the walk in her neighborhood rather than to her anxious thoughts. She felt more confident and ready to tackle an outing to the library.

As you practice tackling items on your hierarchy, remember that each step you take is a success and these small successes will build on each other. The more you practice, the faster you will see your anxiety decrease and your confidence increase. It is extremely helpful to combine the cognitive strategies you have learned with your therapeutic exposure practices to tackle the anxiety-provoking thoughts that will pop up. As you challenge the thoughts and develop a more balanced perspective, it will be easier to stay in situations and feel more comfortable. Eventually, you will know that you have practiced enough when you are more focused on what is going on around you and less focused on your anxiety.

Now create your own exposure hierarchy using Table 7.3 along with a plan for what you will practice first. For each practice, complete the exposure practice learning form (Form 7.5), writing down your anxious thoughts immediately before the practice and what you learned immediately after the practice.

Table 7.3 My Hierarchy of Feared Situations	
Situations	*Anxiety Level (0–100)*

My Plan

_____

_____

_____

Therapeutic Exposure Form: *Zoë's Example*

Situation I Will Practice: <u>Let my partner bathe our daughter in the infant tub while I watch</u>

Before Practice	*After Practice*
Anxiety Level (0–100): <u>45</u>	*Anxiety Level (0–100):* <u>20</u>
Anxious thoughts/ predictions about exposure practice I fear something bad will happen or, at the very least, he will make mistakes and the baby will be upset and cry uncontrollably.	**What actually happened during the exposure?** He did it! It might have been a little clumsier than me, but he did OK. She seemed to enjoy it as she was splashing and they were both laughing. **What did you learn from this experience?** With practice he is learning how he has to hold her and wash her and I am learning that he is capable and nothing bad happens. **What can you take from this experience to help you next time you practice this situation?** I am going to let them have regular bath nights during the week. This will give me some time on my own to have a tea, read a magazine, or watch a half-hour sit-com. They are doing just fine.

Form 7.4   Therapeutic Exposure Form: *Zoë's Example*

Therapeutic Exposure Form

Situation I Will Practice:_____

Before Practice *Anxiety Level (0–100):* _____	*After Practice* *Anxiety Level (0–100):* _____
Anxious thoughts/predictions about exposure practice	What actually happened during the exposure? What did you learn from this experience? What can you take from this experience to help you next time you practice this situation?

Form 7.5 Therapeutic Exposure Form

Activity for Practice

Over the next week, plan to solidify the creation of your hierarchy of feared situations. Next, develop a plan for what you would like to tackle first, second, and so on. Finally, plan to practice a therapeutic exposure multiple times a day or multiple times a week, depending on the therapeutic exposure you have decided on. Remember to document your practice using the exposure form.

Summing It All Up

In the first part of this book, you learned to identify and challenge unhelpful thoughts that were contributing to your anxiety. You also learned to develop more helpful and more balanced thoughts that can decrease distress and promote a greater sense of confidence. In this chapter, we turned to a more behavioral approach to tackling anxiety. Specifically, you learned about a therapeutic exposure-based approach, in which you generated an exposure hierarchy. The idea behind this approach is that avoidance of situations that are associated with anxiety tends to maintain or prolong anxiety in the long run. A better approach is to gradually experiment with entering into, and staying in, situations that make you feel anxious, but in a gradual and systematic manner that is under your control. This gradual exposure gives you the chance to become used to being in these situations (i.e., habituation curve) and to challenge any catastrophic thoughts about the outcomes. Using this approach has the potential to help you build your self-confidence and the sense that you can cope in difficult situations.

References

Abramowitz, J. S., & Moore, E. L. (2007). An experimental analysis of hypochondriasis. *Behaviour Research and Therapy*, *45*, 413–424. doi:10.1016/j.brat.2006.04.005

Beesdo-Baum, K., Jenjahn, E., Hofler, M., Lueken, U., Becker, E.S., & Hoyer, J. (2012). Avoidance, safety behavior, and reassurance-seeking in generalized anxiety disorder. *Depression and Anxiety*, *29*, 948–957.

Salkovskis, P. M. (1991). The importance of behaviour in the maintenance of anxiety and panic: A cognitive account. *Behavioural and Cognitive Psychotherapy*, *19*, 6–19. doi:10.1017/S0141347300011472

Chapter 8

Behavioral Activation

Improving Mood by Changing Behavior

What Is Depression-Related Behavior?

What Is Behavioral Activation?

What Is Paced Respiration?

Social isolation and withdrawal from activities are two of the most common and problematic depression-related behaviors. Isolating oneself or withdrawing from activities, particularly activities that used to bring a sense of pleasure, enjoyment, or satisfaction, can actually reduce the chance of experiencing positive feelings throughout the day. There are a few reasons why people who feel depressed tend to isolate themselves or withdraw from activities. The lack of energy that typically comes with depression can contribute to feeling too tired to participate in an activity, even when it has typically been something that a person has found enjoyable in the past. Also, when depressed, people often believe that they will not experience the *same* amount of pleasure or enjoyment as they have in the past. When this occurs, a person might have the thought 'Why bother if I do not enjoy it as much as I used to?' which can easily stop one from following through. Further, depression may lead to *believing* that these activities will bring no pleasure at all, given that the person is feeling depressed.

When a person is feeling depressed, tired, and low in motivation, the tendency to want to pull back on activities makes sense. However, social isolation and withdrawal can actually make depressive symptoms *worse* over time. Looking at the cognitive behavioral therapy (CBT) model again (Figure 8.1) and thinking about Juanita's example from Chapter 1, we can see why. Juanita had experienced both depression and anxiety in the past and was worried that, once her second child is born, she will be so focused on the daily tasks and responsibilities of caring for two children, that she will become overwhelmed and her depression will return. Being 8 months pregnant, Juanita is indeed

116

starting to struggle with a low mood as she is not participating in her usual hikes and regular get togethers with friends. She fears that this lack of balance of activities will become more of a problem with the challenge of managing the needs of both children when her second baby is born. Juanita remembers that it takes more energy to carry out daily tasks and that she is not as able to enjoy activities that she once enjoyed. Feeling depressed, overwhelmed, and discouraged can increase fatigue or lethargy and when Juanita thinks about engaging in activities that bring her a sense of pleasure (e.g., lunch with a friend, going for a hike), she might be more likely to think 'I'm too overwhelmed to take time for myself' or 'Why bother? I won't enjoy it anyway' in the postpartum. Although Juanita's identified feelings are accurate (e.g., depressed, overwhelmed), her thoughts are predictions that she will not get *any* enjoyment from lunch with a friend, going for a hike, or even taking a moment to have a cup of tea.

We know, however, that people who are depressed often underestimate the beneficial impact that these types of activities can have on their mood. By not engaging in her usual pleasurable activities, Juanita does not give herself the chance to experience *any* pleasure or satisfaction from these activities. As a result, she may begin to feel even more isolated and overwhelmed, which in turn may make her mood worse. In other words, the very behaviors that we tend to engage in when feeling depressed can actually exacerbate depressive symptoms. As Figure 8.1 suggests, in order to change negative feelings we need to change behavior.

It is both necessary and important to acknowledge that changes in behavior naturally occur during pregnancy and the postpartum (e.g., no longer engaging in

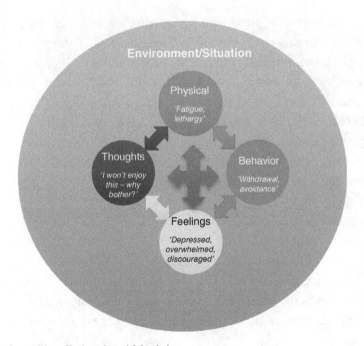

Figure 8.1   Cognitive Behavioral Model

exercise like running, stopping work and staying at home with the baby). Priorities naturally change as well and new mothers often have *less* time for activities that brought them 'balance,' activities that they previously found pleasurable or satisfying. However, making sure that activities that help boost your mood are at least part of your weekly routine can be an important step in improving mood or reducing the risk of depressive symptoms in the future.

Behavioral Activation

The main focus of this chapter is targeting depression with a strategy called *behavioral activation* (BA). BA is a powerful treatment strategy for depression that has been found to be very effective, even in the long term. Interestingly, people who respond to pharmacotherapy for depression have been found to relapse at higher rates when they withdraw from their medication compared to those who have engaged in behavioral activation (Dimidjian et al., 2006; Dobson et al., 2008). BA involves a strategic approach to adding activities into a person's day-to-day life that have a good chance of improving mood or adding a sense of satisfaction. That stated, it is never a good idea to just start adding in random activities. Having a strategy, particularly in the perinatal period, is important to maximize the benefit that is gained from each activity. Activities that can have a beneficial impact on mood are not always activities that bring a sense of pleasure. Activities that bring a sense of *satisfaction* can also have a significant beneficial impact on mood (e.g., doing the laundry or paying bills). They might not be pleasurable on their own but can feel good and increase a sense of accomplishment when getting them done.

Engaging in BA as a strategy during pregnancy and the postpartum period requires important consideration of the unique perinatal context that a woman is in. The biological and physical impact of pregnancy and the postpartum period results in lower levels of energy, especially in the final months of pregnancy and early postpartum. Physical discomfort during pregnancy (e.g., nausea in the early months, backache in the later months) and in the early postpartum (e.g., recovery from delivery or a cesarean section) may mean that physical activity will need to be temporarily reduced. Further, if a new mother is waking repeatedly at night to feed her baby, sleep deprivation can occur and sabotage best efforts of planned activities for the next day.

Another significant and unique context of the perinatal period is the increased focus on childcare and household care of a new mother. This often means that new mothers have much less time to engage in other pleasurable activities than in the past. Even the financial changes that often occur with the arrival of a new baby can place limits on the types of pleasurable activities that a woman can engage in. This chapter addresses the use of BA in the unique context of the perinatal period.

The first step is to identify these activities. Use Form 8.1 to start brainstorming possible pleasurable or satisfying activities. These are activities that either used to or currently bring you pleasure or enjoyment when you engage in them. An important note when identifying these activities is to have a range of activities that are considered small, medium, and large. Large activities are ones that take a fair amount of time, organizing, or resources to engage in (e.g., going on a weekend trip to visit family a couple hours away). Small activities take relatively little time or resources. Having activities that vary in how much time, energy, or resources they take will give you a broader range of options for times when you are feeling depressed, tired, or overwhelmed.

List of Pleasurable or Enjoyable Activities

Small Activities	Medium Activities	Large Activities
Sit for 5 minutes with a cup of tea	Make a simple but tasty lunch	Make dinner from a new recipe
Read a short magazine article	Read a chapter in your favourite book	Read several chapters in a new book
Watch a TV program with your partner when the kids are in bed	Go for a walk with your partner	Plan a 'date night' with your partner
_____	_____	_____
_____	_____	_____
_____	_____	_____
_____	_____	_____
_____	_____	_____

Form 8.1 List of Activities

List of Activities That Bring About a Sense of Satisfaction or Accomplishment

Small Activities	Medium Activities	Large Activities
Clean the kitchen counter	Clean the kitchen	Clean the house
Find the bills that need paying	Check the bank statements	Pay bills
Go for a 10-minute brisk walk	Go for a 20-minute jog	Go to the gym/yoga class
_____	_____	_____
_____	_____	_____
_____	_____	_____
_____	_____	_____
_____	_____	_____
_____	_____	_____

Form 8.1 *(continued)*

Taking Action with Scheduling Activities

After a number of activities have been identified and listed in Form 8.1, the next step is to start engaging in some of these activities by strategically inserting them into your day. Importantly, when planning activities, one size does not fit all. For instance, gardening might be very pleasurable for some women and promote happiness and joy, while others might dislike working in the yard and see it as a chore. Therefore, it is important to be strategic and engage in activities that have a higher chance of giving you pleasure or a sense of satisfaction.

It is possible that participating in an activity that *used to* bring you pleasure does not have the same impact as before. However, it is important not to discard the activity after a single attempt! Instead, try it out a few times in different ways to see if doing it really can have a positive impact or not. An important component to the strategy behind activity scheduling, particularly in pregnancy and postpartum, is to keep in mind your current level of energy, mood, and other resources at a given point in time. A woman who is exhausted because she is feeding her infant throughout the night may not be able to go to the gym for a vigorous workout the next morning. Instead, a brief but brisk walk during the day while the baby is in the stroller may be much more realistic. Similarly, a women who is experiencing considerable fatigue and low mood may find going out for lunch with friends too difficult but might benefit significantly from planning a chat with a friend by phone. The idea is to plan activities that provide a benefit to your mood but that take your energy and limited time into account in a realistic way.

Use Form 8.2 to help schedule activities and to track your experience when trying out new activities over the next few weeks. An important saying in the process of BA, especially when feeling down or depressed is, *follow the plan – not the mood*. We know that when people feel depressed they tend to wait until they feel motivated before taking action. However, if we wait for that feeling to arrive it may never come and we never get the benefit of the activity. Looking at the CBT model in Figure 8.1 again, reducing activities can turn into a vicious cycle, leading to lower motivation, less activity, more depression, less motivation, and so on. Remember that it is important to start small. Change will come more easily this way as a small activity is usually easier to engage in. This can be hard for someone who is used to doing a lot all of the time. The goal here is balance in a way that makes sense during pregnancy and the postpartum when schedules are already full and it seems like every hour is accounted for with activities.

Once you have generated a list of pleasurable or satisfying activities, the next step is to select one or two to start with. Planning these activities at a time when your mood might be somewhat low is a strategic way to begin. For instance, if you know that your mood tends to be lower in the mornings, that might be an ideal time for a cup of tea. If your mood is low in the evenings, you might want to negotiate with your family so that you can have a bath while your partner looks after the children.

Finally, tracking the benefits of each activity on your mood is important in helping you identify which activities you will want to continue to add and which ones might be less beneficial for your mood. Form 8.2 provides guidelines on how to monitor the impact of a given activity on your mood. Before you engage in the activity, make note of the activity and when you plan to engage in it. Next, rate how much pleasure or satisfaction you expect to gain from the activity. Because we know that people who are depressed tend to underestimate the benefits of activities on mood, testing these predictions is an important part of this process. Finally, once you have engaged in the activity, how much pleasure or satisfaction did you actually experience? Was it more or less than you expected? If so, why? If you experienced less pleasure or satisfaction, what would you want to do differently the next time you try the activity to see whether it can have a benefit on your mood? Make any notes that you would like to remember in the 'Comments' column.

Activity Mood-Monitoring Form: 'Expected Versus Actual'

Rate how much pleasure/enjoyment/satisfaction you 'expect' to derive from the planned activity prior to engaging in it. Following the completion of the activity, re-rate the 'actual' amount of pleasure/enjoyment/satisfaction you derived from it.

Day of Week	Activity	How much Pleasure/ Satisfaction You 'Expect'	How much 'Actual' Pleasure/ Satisfaction Received	Comments
Saturday night	Date night with husband. Leaving son with grand-parents	2	6	Tired and hectic before we left; started to relax and enjoy myself once we got to the restaurant

Form 8.2 Activity Mood-Monitoring Form

The Power of Exercise as Part of Behavioral Activation

Research has confirmed that exercise has multiple benefits that extend from enhancing your mood and fitness to improving your quality of life. Therefore, as you add new activities into your schedule it is worthwhile considering adding in a form of exercise. Of course, everyone is different in terms of activity level and physical restrictions. If you are unsure about what level or type of exercise would be appropriate for you, start with a walk and then further discuss with your doctor or healthcare professional.

Although going to the gym or for a jog are often the types of activities that most people think of when planning to increase their level of physical activity, these are not always options given the changes in lifestyle that often accompany having a new baby (e.g., financial changes, fatigue, not having childcare for an infant). Fortunately, there are many other options that can be more feasible for women during the perinatal period. Walking with a friend while pushing the baby in a baby stroller, yoga classes for mothers and infants, or exercise classes that allow infants in community centers are often options. Although it can take some phone calls to locate these types of activities in your area, there are many benefits in addition to exercise, including the opportunity for new or expecting mothers to connect with and share experiences with other mothers. In fact, because we know that new motherhood can be an isolating time for women who are at home with their baby, adding social activities is extremely important to your list of pleasurable or satisfying activities.

Paced Respiration: One More Important Behavioral Tool

One final behavioral tool will be introduced here. Paced respiration is a strategy that can target physical tension and emotional distress fairly directly and can be applied when a person is feeling a range of negative emotions, including anxiety, panic, frustration, anger, or even sadness. As you'll see, paced respiration can help to reduce anxiety or panic by changing the way you might be breathing in situations in which your 'fight or flight' response has been activated. Paced respiration may also help to reduce distress by helping you focus on something that is neutral (i.e., your breathing) when you are feeling any number of negative emotions and experiencing a range of negative thinking patterns (e.g., worry, rumination).

Paced respiration is a slow, controlled diaphragmatic breathing technique. The goal with paced respiration is to replace chest breathing, which is quick and shallow, with slow, deep, abdominal breathing. This type of breathing has primarily been used to help reduce anxiety or tension. With deep abdominal breathing, your diaphragm moves downward and causes your belly to rise. With shallow breathing, your chest and shoulders will rise. One way to determine if you are presently engaged in *chest* or *belly* breathing is to place one hand on your chest, the other on your belly, and pay attention to which hand rises as you breathe normally. If the hand on your chest rises more, you are engaged in chest breathing. If the hand on your belly rises more, you are engaged in belly breathing.

The next exercise will help you learn to breathe from your diaphragm, using paced respiration (Figure 8.2), to target the severity as well as the duration of your anxiety or distress. This approach may also help to reduce other types of negative emotion (e.g., frustration, anger).

Steps for Paced Respiration

1. Inhale slowly through your nose up to a count of 5 (shorter if that is more comfortable). The idea is to exaggerate the inhalation in a slow, controlled way.

2. Pause for a moment.

3. Exhale slowly through your nose up to a count of five (again, shorter if that is more comfortable). The idea is to exaggerate the exhalation in a slow, controlled way.

4. Pause for a moment.

5. Repeat for several cycles.

Try to practice this exercise multiple times throughout the day. Practice initially at times when you are already feeling calm and relaxed. After you become comfortable with this technique, practice it when you sense the early signs of anxiety (or other forms of distress) increasing and continue for as long as you need to. Note that at first it may take some time before the technique leads to a greater sense of calm or relaxation. The more you practice, however, the more efficient and effective this technique tends to be. Use Form 8.3 to track your experience of paced respiration whenever you use it and especially at the first signs of anxiety or distress. Tracking your experience will help you determine whether this behavioral strategy is a helpful and effective one for you.

Record your experience of paced respiration in Form 8.3, including the date and situation in which you practice it. Before using this technique, record your level of distress on a scale of 0–100, where 0 is the least distress/anxiety and 100 is the most distress/anxiety you could feel. Using the same scale, record the level of distress/anxiety after your practice. Finally, record your experience of paced respiration after practicing it, including any thoughts or feelings you noticed as you were using the strategy.

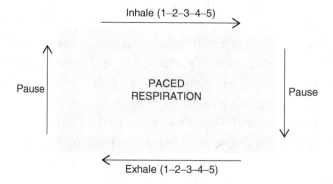

Figure 8.2 Paced Respiration

Date and Situation	Distress/ Anxiety Before (0–100)	Distress/Anxiety After (0–100)	Comments About Your Practice
	8	4	Distress did not go away completely, but paced respiration helped reduce it and gave me a moment to think clearly instead of just react

Form 8.3 Paced Respiration Record Form

Summing It All Up

This chapter introduced the technique of BA. Depression-related behaviors include withdrawal or isolation from others and reduction in the number and variety of day-to-day activities that we engage in. Although low energy and motivation can contribute to depressive symptoms, withdrawal and isolation can increase and maintain depressive symptoms over time. Because the perinatal period is a time of heightened risk for depression, it is imperative to plan and engage in activities that are likely to improve your mood. However, this strategy must take into account the changes that occur in women's lives during pregnancy and with the addition of a new baby. These include changes in energy levels, physical discomfort, and lifestyle changes.

This chapter provides an overview and guidance on engaging in BA, specifically during the unique perinatal context. Finally, this chapter introduces another behavioral technique – paced respiration – that can be used to reduce anxiety, panic, or other negative emotions, including frustration, anger, or even low mood.

References

Dimidjian, S., Hollon, S. D., Dobson, K. S., Schmaling, K. B., Kohlenberg, R. J., Addis, M. E., ... & Jacobson, N. S. (2006). Randomized trial of behavioral activation, cognitive therapy, and antidepressant medication in the acute treatment of adults with major depression. *Journal of Consulting and Clinical Psychology, 74*, 658–670.

Dobson, K. S., Hollon, S. D., Dimidjian, S., Schmaling, K. B., Kohlenberg, R. J., Gallop, R., ... Jacobson, N. S. (2008). Randomized trial of behavioral activation, cognitive therapy, and antidepressant medication in the prevention of relapse and recurrence in major depression. *Journal of Consulting and Clinical Psychology, 76*, 468–477.

Chapter 9

Assertive Communication

*Developing the Skills to Attain
Your Needs*

What Is Assertive Communication?

Why Is Assertiveness Important During Pregnancy and the Postpartum?

How Do I Increase My Assertive Communication Skills?

In this last treatment chapter, we will be focusing on *assertiveness* and *assertive communication*. As human beings we are constantly communicating with one another. When you let someone know your opinion, when you say 'no' to a request, or when you ask for something that you need, you are engaging in assertive communication. Many people think of assertiveness as a fixed personality trait (e.g., 'I'm just not an assertive person'). However, assertiveness is actually *a set of communication skills* rather than a personality style you are born with. Importantly, assertive communication skills can be learned and mastered with practice just like any other set of skills. In this chapter, you will learn about different styles of communication (i.e., assertive, passive, aggressive, passive-aggressive), the importance of assertive communication during pregnancy and the postpartum period, and strategies to increase your ability to communicate more assertively.

What Is Assertive Communication?

Assertive communication involves expressing your feelings, needs, and opinions in an open and direct manner while at the same time respecting the feelings, opinions, and needs of others. For example, you might want to make a direct request or respond to a criticism while not coming across as overly defensive or hostile. Assertive communication is *not* about always getting your way or making sure that *only* your needs are considered. It is also not about forcing others to change their behavior. In fact, assertive communication often involves openness to negotiation and collaboration with the person you are communicating with – just not at the expense of your own rights or needs. Although communicating assertively does not guarantee that you will always get what you want, this approach can significantly increase the chance that you will.

The Importance of Assertive Communication During Pregnancy and the Postpartum Period

Many challenges occur during pregnancy and the postpartum period. A great deal of preparation occurs prior to the baby's arrival. In addition, you have a significant number of new responsibilities in the postpartum period, often while experiencing uncomfortable physical changes and reduced sleep. For these reasons, it is essential to access and make good use of your sources of social support. In fact, we know that if you feel that you have good social support during pregnancy, you are significantly less likely to experience mental health difficulties both in pregnancy and in the postpartum period (Gjerdingen et al., 1991; Negron et al., 2013).

Consider Juanita's example from Chapters 1 and 2 and how the lack of support she had was having such a negative impact on her anxiety and depression. Researchers have found that women who receive greater physical support (e.g., completing day-to-day tasks) and emotional support (e.g., receiving caring and empathy from others) report better mental health during their pregnancy and the postpartum period than women with less support (Gjerdingen et al., 1991). Women who receive greater informational support during pregnancy (e.g., prenatal classes that offer facts about pregnancy and the postpartum) also have better physical and mental health in the early postpartum period compared to women who receive less support.

This research really highlights the importance of activating your resource and support systems. Acting assertively can pose a challenge for many women – particularly for those who struggle with anxiety and depression, and for those who have had difficulties with assertiveness in the past. In addition, women can vary in their comfort with asking for help. Quite often women are the ones helping and caring for those around them (or are expected to do so), so it may be difficult to step up and ask for support for themselves. We have also found that some women hold beliefs that get in the way of asking for help in an assertive way when help is needed. For example, common beliefs include the idea that 'Other mothers are able to manage all of the increased responsibilities and challenges without asking for help, I should be able to do so as well,' or 'Others will think I can't handle this or I will fall short as a mother if I ask for help.' Notice the thinking errors in these beliefs (all or nothing, mind reading). If these beliefs are familiar to you, you may be reluctant to seek help and these beliefs will need to be challenged and turned into more helpful thoughts.

In general, seeking greater support may involve asking your partner, members of your family and friends, or members of medical or mental health services for help in a variety of ways. The assertiveness skills you will learn in this chapter will help you to maximize the availability of support and resources you have. The first step in developing your assertive communication skills is to understand and recognize the other three main types of communication: passive, aggressive, and passive-aggressive.

Passive Communication

In *passive* communication, the goal is usually to avoid conflict (e.g., 'I just won't say anything because it will end up in a fight'), avoid rejection (e.g., 'If I express a different opinion from everyone else's, I will end up being excluded'), or please others (e.g., 'I don't want to disappoint everyone so I will agree to the request'). Passive communication includes always saying '*yes*' to requests even when they are inappropriate, agreeing with others even when you disagree, or never directly expressing your needs (and hoping that others will guess what they are). Both verbal and non-verbal passive communication tells others (often unintentionally) that your needs or opinions do not matter or that others' needs or opinions are more important.

Although the goal in passive communication may be to avoid harming important relationships, engaging in this type of communication may lead you to feel anxious, hurt, or frustrated. There is also the risk of feeling increasingly resentful toward others if your needs are not met and you feel taken advantage of. The individuals you are communicating with may also feel confusion and frustration. Given that frequent use of passive communication is associated with poor mental health, including lower self-esteem (Sarkova et al., 2013), and an increased risk of depressive symptoms (Segal, 2005), learning a more assertive communication style is important for your sense of well-being.

Aggressive Communication

In contrast to *passive* communication, the goal in *aggressive* communication is to control or dominate a situation. This usually involves imposing your own needs and opinions on others, without respecting or acknowledging others' needs or feelings. Both verbal and non-verbal aggressive communication tells others that *your* needs matter in that moment and that the other person's needs do not. At the extreme, aggressive communication can involve threats or verbal attacks on others (e.g., 'If you don't start helping maybe we should just get a divorce'). Although individuals engaging in this type of communication may see it as a way to get what they want, interacting with someone who is routinely aggressive in their communication can lead others to feel hurt, upset, defensive, angry, or humiliated.

It should be noted here that people who engage in aggressive communication may not always intend to do so. They may see their communication style as the result of a specific circumstance, rather than a problematic pattern of responding, and may not realize the impact it has on others. If this is true for you, learning assertiveness skills to communicate effectively is just as important as it is for those who struggle with a more passive approach.

Passive-Aggressive Communication

A *passive-aggressive* approach to communication combines the reluctance toward expressing your needs or opinions directly, as we see in the passive approach, with the anger or hostility observed in an aggressive approach. Individuals engaging in this type of communication may be afraid of the consequences of being open about their true thoughts or feelings and will instead express these opinions, including anger or hostility, in less direct ways. Interestingly, the 'passive' portion of the communication (e.g., agreeing to a task you do not actually intend to complete or agreeing with others' opinions when you actually disagree) is often expressed verbally, whereas the 'aggressive' portion is often expressed non-verbally (e.g., rolling your eyes as you agree to complete a task, 'forgetting' to do a task you have agreed to, or muttering loudly and angrily while you complete a task that you were asked to do). Giving someone the 'silent treatment' – or refusing to speak openly about how you feel while also providing clear non-verbal cues that you are upset or angry – is another example of passive-aggressive behavior (e.g., agreeing to do the laundry, with a sigh, and then stomping up the stairs with the laundry basket).

In each case, there are two contradictory messages being conveyed. The message that is conveyed non-verbally (i.e., with the sighing loudly and stomping up the stairs) is the one that tends to stand out. Although this type of communication may be powerful from an emotional point of view, it tends to be much less effective in helping you meet your needs compared to an assertive approach and can cause other problems in your relationships. Individuals who are on the receiving end of this type of communication may feel confused, hurt, angry, or manipulated (e.g., 'She agreed to do the laundry, saying it would not be a problem, so why is she sighing and stomping loudly up the stairs? Did I do something wrong?').

Tips to Distinguish between Assertive, Passive, and Aggressive Behavior

The most obvious component of assertive communication is what you say or the *verbal* component. Assertive language tends to be firm and direct rather than involving hesitant, lengthy, or indirect statements. Table 9.1 lists some of the main verbal characteristics of assertive communication.

Non-verbal communication (i.e., your body language) is also a crucial component of communication. Your body language, including your posture, facial expressions, and gestures, communicates important information to others and can help – or hinder – the message you want to deliver. Table 9.2 includes examples of non-verbal characteristics of assertive communication.

Table 9.1 Assertive Verbal Characteristics

Use of clear, brief, and direct statements	'I would like you to …' 'I think that …' 'I won't be able to …'
An *honest* reflection of your thoughts, feelings, or needs	'I need your help with …' 'I'm feeling angry right now' 'I'm not happy with …'
A high proportion of 'I' statements that focus on *your* experience	'I think that ____ is really interesting' 'I feel anxious when you …' 'I appreciate it when you …'
Use of objective language, rather than making assumptions about what others think or feel	'My impression is that you find this task challenging, is that right?'

Table 9.2 Assertive Non-Verbal (Behavioral) Characteristics

Tone of voice and volume	Firm, steady, and often warm tone, loud enough to hear comfortably without having to strain or step back
Eye contact	Steady, direct, and relaxed gaze with occasional glances away (as is typical during everyday speech), not overly staring
Stance and posture	Facing the listener with an open stance (e.g., upright and relaxed posture, leaning forward a little but not into the other person's personal space)
Hands	Relaxed hand movements that add to, rather than distract from, what you are saying

Passive Communication

Passive communication conveys the idea that your opinions and needs are *less important* than others' opinions and needs. Passive verbal communication tends to involve hesitant, overly long sentences with many words that are unrelated to the point you are trying to make (e.g., um, ah, so, well). Table 9.3 provides some examples of passive verbal communication.

Passive communication behaviors include facial expressions, postures, and gestures that emphasize your own uncertainty about what you are saying or that what you are saying is not important. Examples of passive behavioral communication are described in Table 9.4.

Aggressive Communication

In aggressive communication, the goal is often to control the situation or communicate the idea that your needs are more important than others' needs. Aggressive verbal communication tends to involve blunt, direct statements with words that are critical, accusing, or expressing strong negative emotions. Examples of aggressive communication are provided in Table 9.5.

Aggressive non-verbal communication conveys a powerful message that others' opinions and needs do not matter. Examples of behaviors that often occur during aggressive communication are listed in Table 9.6 and are consistent with efforts to try to control the situation or to impose one's ideas or opinions on others.

In the next sections, you will learn a number of skills and strategies to help you develop a more assertive style of communication so that you can get the help that you need. The first step, however, is to identify the situations in which you have difficulty being assertive. In Form 9.1, write down each situation in which assertive communication has been a challenge. Reflect on what thoughts or beliefs might be contributing to your lack of assertiveness in each situation and write them down. Use Juanita's, Elizabeth's, and Zoë's examples below as a guide.

Juanita's Example

Situation: I will have difficulty asking others for help when the baby arrives, including my mother and sisters.

Thoughts/Beliefs: They are very busy and I do not want to burden them further by asking for their help. Like others, I should be able to manage on my own.

Elizabeth's Example

Situation: I feel the need for more balance in my daily activities, such as going for a run or coffee with a friend without the baby, but I do not ask for the help that would allow me to do this.

Table 9.3 Passive Verbal Characteristics

Use of hesitant, overly long sentences without a clear point, or use of words that express uncertainty or apology for what you are saying	'Would it be OK if you, well, um . . . only if it works for you of course, and ah . . .' 'I'm sorry to ask but . . .' (when it is a reasonable request)
Avoiding making a clear statement when there is one you would like to make	'I don't really know . . .' (when you do) 'I might be able to do that for you, maybe . . .' (when you know you really can't)
Making assumptions about what others think or feel in a way that reflects poorly on *you*	'I know you probably don't want to do this but . . .' 'I know this is silly but could you . . .'

Table 9.4 Passive Non-Verbal (Behavioral) Characteristics

Tone of voice and volume	Hesitant, shaky, and full of pauses, and often too quiet to be heard comfortably
Eye contact	Looking away most of the time or little direct eye contact, downcast or pleading expression
Stance and posture	Turned or leaning slightly away from the listener, with a slouched posture (often associated with feelings of helplessness or defeat), or excessive head nodding
Hands	Fluttering, fidgety, or vague hand movements that do not add to (and may distract from) what you are saying

Table 9.5   Aggressive Verbal Characteristics

High frequency of 'you' statements with a focus on blaming others	'You are to blame here . . .' 'This is all your fault . . .'
Dismissive of or minimizing others' needs and opinions	'You want *what*? Well, that doesn't matter . . .' 'You're just being emotional right now, I don't have to listen to you' 'I don't care what you think, I'm usually right anyway'
Making assumptions about what others think or feel in a way that reflects poorly on *them*	'You never know what you're talking about' 'Everyone else agrees with me . . .' (without supporting evidence)
Use of emotionally charged, accusatory, or excessively critical language	'You're an idiot/useless/incompetent' 'You're a terrible spouse/parent/person'

Table 9.6 Aggressive Non-Verbal (Behavioral) Characteristics

Tone of voice and volume	Excessively loud, harsh, or forceful tone, often interrupting or speaking over others, or use of sarcasm to belittle
Eye contact	Excessive, staring eye contact without pause, and a narrowed or 'cold' gaze
Stance and posture	Leaning into the other person's personal space, hands on hips, or stiff and rigid posture
Hands	Clenched hands and abrupt gestures, finger pointing, or fist pounding

Thoughts/Beliefs: <u>Since I am on maternity leave and away from work, I should be the one taking care of all the household chores and childcare all of the time. I should not have to ask for help if this is my job/the agreement.</u>

Zoë's Example

Situation: <u>Whenever a family member calls to say they want to see the baby I drop everything to allow them to come over, even if I have plans, the baby is sleeping, or I am exhausted.</u>

Thoughts/Beliefs: <u>I want to make my family happy by helping them to see the baby. If I say no, they will be disappointed or think that I am preventing them from seeing her. My needs are not as important.</u>

1. Situation:_____

_____

Thoughts/Beliefs:_____

_____

2. Situation:_____

_____

Thoughts/Beliefs:_____

_____

3. Situation:_____

_____

Thoughts/Beliefs:_____

_____

4. Situation:_____

_____

Thoughts/Beliefs: _____

_____

Form 9.1   My Difficulties with Assertiveness

Deciding When to Be Assertive

Assertive communication is often the most effective way to ensure that your needs are met in many situations. However, *not all* situations require assertive communication. In fact, there are times when an assertive approach may *not* be the most appropriate choice. For example, imagine you find yourself in an argument with someone whose opinion you do not share, but where asserting your opinion is not particularly important to you and you know the other person is likely to respond badly (e.g., communicating that you believe basketball is the best sport of all time, not soccer, to an avid soccer fan). Here you might decide to take a more passive approach (e.g., simply smiling and keeping your opinion to yourself). In another situation where you or someone you love is threatened, you may decide that a more aggressive approach is necessary (e.g., yelling to a driver to stop while putting your hand up as you cross the street with your baby). There is nothing inherently wrong with any of these approaches and, in fact, all communication falls on a continuum from passive to aggressive (Figure 9.1).

The decision about whether to engage in assertive communication in a specific situation is a personal one and will depend on how important the situation is to you and whether the benefits of being assertive outweigh any potential negative consequences. Using Form 9.3 (below), evaluate the pros and cons of using an assertive approach in the situations you listed in Form 9.1. Once you have listed the pros and cons, analyze each list to consider how they balance out to determine whether to proceed. Keep your eye out for any thinking errors you may be making and use your cognitive strategies to develop an accurate view. In Form 9.2, you will find Zoë's entry as an example to illustrate the pros and cons she generated as she considered whether to respond in an assertive way when family members call to ask if they can come over to see the new baby and it is not a good time. Notice how she caught the thinking error that really made it more challenging for her to be assertive.

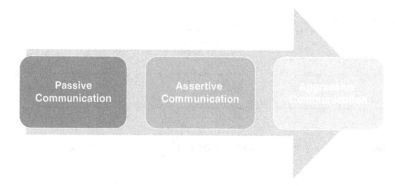

Figure 9.1 Communication Spectrum

Situation: <u>Declining an invitation to visit and suggesting alternative times for</u> <u>my family members to visit my daughter when they call asking to come over.</u>

Cons	Pros
■ They may be upset and disappointed ■ They might tell me 'I never visit' or 'I am keeping them from their grandchild' ■ I will feel guilty	■ I will not disrupt my daughter's nap schedule or other things in her routine ■ This will be less distressing for me because I won't have to change my day, or cancel appointments, and I will still be able to get my errands/ tasks done, such as grocery shopping, making dinner, and going for coffee with a friend ■ We will still be able to visit but at a different day/time. Both parties are getting their needs met this way ■ I might eventually feel more confident if I practice assertive communication in this situation ■ I will feel good about myself because I will be putting my daughter's needs first

Form 9.2 Weighing Pros and Cons of Assertive Communication: *Zoë's Example*

Zoë's Reflection: *Although my family members may be disappointed, it will be better overall for me and the baby if we can plan another time. This approach will be uncomfortable for me but with practice it will be easier. My family is actually quite reasonable and I doubt they will really feel that I am keeping them from their grandchild (catastrophizing!) when I schedule an alternate time to visit.*

Situation:_____

_____

Cons	Pros

Reflection:_____

_____

Form 9.3   Weighing Pros and Cons of Assertive Communication

Being Strategic: Planning for Effective Assertive Communication

Once you have identified the situation in which you would like to practice assertive communication, the next step is to develop a concrete plan. It may seem odd to plan this in advance. Remember, we are working to create circumstances that increase the likelihood that you will be able to act assertively and in which others are likely to hear your message and respond in a way that meets your needs. Take a moment to consider the following: when are *you* most likely to respond well to another person's assertive communication? If you are like most people, it is not when you are tired, overwhelmed, or already upset. Asking someone for more help with household care, for example, may not be effective if the request is made just after your partner has arrived home from work, the children are crying, and you are both exhausted. The first step in planning effective assertive communication is to choose the best *person, time,* and *place.*

Choosing the Right Person

The right person is someone who is in a position to provide what you need. Communicating assertively with a friend about the help you need from your partner with household care is not likely to help you get that help, although it may help you with planning your approach. Speaking directly with your partner or other family members is likely to be more effective. Some individuals also respond better to assertive communication than others and so you may want to start with someone who you believe is more likely to respond well to your request.

Choosing the Right Time

Choosing the moment just after everyone gets home for the day, right in the middle of making dinner, may not be the most effective time. Try to choose a time when everyone is more relaxed and less distracted. This might take some planning (e.g., hiring a babysitter for the children, planning a time when the children are occupied or in bed).

Choosing the Right Place

What is the best location for your communication? It might not be while out in a grocery store or when there are others around who might interfere with your message. For some situations, a quiet, private place is ideal because it allows you and the other person to express your thoughts openly. For other situations, a public setting might be best if you are concerned about how the other person might respond.

Consider the situation you have chosen: who would it be best to speak with? When and where would you like this conversation to take place? Form 9.4 allows you to plan these things in a concrete way. Zoë's example is described in Form 9.5.

Situation	Why I choose this person/time/place
1. Best person:	1.
2. Best time:	2.
3. Best place:	3.

Form 9.4 Best Person, Time, and Place

Situation: Speak to in-laws about visiting	Why I choose this person/time/place
1. **Best person:** Mother-in-law	1. She respects and cares about me and has been understanding in the past, such as when I told her I would just like my partner in the delivery room
2. **Best time:** On the weekend when my partner is also home	2. Everyone is more relaxed on the weekend and my partner can help watch the baby while I speak to my mother-in-law
3. **Best place:** In the kitchen when my partner is watching the baby with my father-in-law	3. We won't be distracted or interrupted by the baby and it will be quiet

Form 9.5   Best Person, Time, and Place: *Zoë's Example*

Next Steps: Clarify Your Goals

Clarifying your goals prior to communicating assertively is an essential step that is often overlooked. There may be situations in which your goals are clear (e.g., to ask your partner to take on an additional household task each week). However, if communication in your family occurs when everyone is distracted or when emotions are running high, your goals may be more difficult to identify. In fact, when feeling upset, our goal is usually to do something (anything!) to feel less upset in that moment (e.g., snapping at a loved one) rather than to solve a longer-term problem or to have an important need met (e.g., getting more help with household care).

Take a moment to consider the situation you identified in the previous section. What would you like to accomplish? What need are you hoping to have met? Try to identify goals that are *specific, concrete*, and *measurable*. For instance, if your goal is to have your partner 'be a better partner,' how will he or she know where to start? This goal is too vague and also carries a hidden statement that your partner is *never* a good partner. In this example, it would be more effective to select specific things that your partner could do to help you meet your needs (e.g., take responsibility for making meals several nights a week or take the children on an outing on the weekends to give you time to rest or do other needed activities). The more concrete and specific a goal is in terms of behavior (i.e., what the other person can *do* differently), the more likely you are to have the goal met. Both Zoë's and Elizabeth's goals are provided below to illustrate this.

Zoë's Assertive Goal

Goal: To decide on a time for a visit that works best for everyone instead of dropping everything when someone calls with a request to come over and visit.

Measurable: Unplanned visiting happens about six times a week on average. My goal is to reduce how often this happens to twice per week at most so the majority of visits are planned at times that work for me and the baby.

Elizabeth's Assertive Goal

Goal: To ask for more help with childcare several times each week so that I can engage in some of my other activities more often, such as getting exercise and going for coffee with a friend.

Measurable: I only have 'me time' about once a week, usually when my husband asks me if I want him to watch our daughter. This needs to increase and I would like to ask him to watch her on two other occasions in the week.

My Assertive Goal

Goal: _____

_____

Measurable (i.e., how will you know you met this goal?): _____

_____

Planning What to Say: Building an Assertiveness Script

You have put in a great deal of preparation into your plan for assertive communication at this point, including selecting the right person, time, and place, and identifying your goal. However, what will you actually say when you decide to communicate assertively? Here, too, we strongly recommend that you plan ahead. Thinking of how to state your needs in a moment when distress is high is certainly not ideal and can actually be very challenging. Having a script prepared ahead of time can help you stick to your goal and ensure that your communication is as clear as possible. The following steps will help you to develop your assertiveness script.

Start With an Empathy Statement

The first step in planning what you will say is to develop an empathy statement. This may seem surprising because the goal of an empathy statement is to acknowledge *the other person's needs or opinions*. Remember, however, that assertive communication involves asserting your own needs while respecting others' needs. If others feel that their needs are acknowledged, they are less likely to become defensive and more willing to listen to what you have to say. The empathy statement reflects the aspects of the person's behavior that you genuinely appreciate and may want to maintain. This statement, of course, needs to be honest – the goal is not to manipulate others or to present a view that you do not hold. In Zoë's example above, her empathy statement could sound like, 'I really appreciate how much you come over to visit with us and the baby. I can tell how much you love her and I appreciate the help you provide when you are here.'

Develop a Basic Assertion

The next step is to develop a clear statement about: (1) *how* you feel; (2) *when* you feel this way; and (3) *why*. Assertive communication generally involves brief, direct statements with a clear point and does not include accusatory language. The focus is on how *you* feel (e.g., anxious, frustrated, sad, overwhelmed), using an 'I' statement. Focusing on how you feel can be effective because it avoids blaming or accusing words (e.g., 'You never do this right!'). In addition, a basic assertion can include an explanation as to *when* and *why* you feel the way you do. This is not a justification of how you feel but involves offering a brief explanation of the specific circumstances that lead you to feel this way. To help you get started, a general format might include the following:

1. 'I feel _____ '
2. 'when you_____ '
3. 'because_____ '

Zoë's Example,

1. 'I feel <u>anxious</u>'
2. 'When <u>you call saying you are in the neighborhood and are on your way over</u>'
3. 'Because <u>things are often hectic for us in the evenings.</u>'

Indicate What You Would Like to Be Different

Next, identify what you would like the other person to change. Here, too, being specific and focusing on concrete behaviors will be more effective than a vague or critical statement. Asking a person to 'be a better partner' is too vague (where does the individual start?). Instead, identify one or two specific and concrete behaviors you would like the other person to change. This statement might take the form of the following: 'I would like you to_____.'

Zoë's Example
'It would be really helpful for me if we planned your visits in advance. I would like you to come over next Saturday or Sunday afternoon as it works well for the baby and us. Would that work for you?'

End With Another Empathy Statement (Optional)

If you feel it is appropriate and you think the other person may not be happy with your request, adding another empathy statement can be helpful at this point. This statement, of course, must be honest and acknowledge the other person's response, without deviating from your goal.

Zoë's Example

> I know this might not have been what you were hoping to hear because you like to pop by. Having you over on the weekends means we will be better able to enjoy the time that we spend with you because we will be less distracted and exhausted.

Keep in mind that the script offered above involves suggestions and will need to be modified according to what you think will work best given your situation and how others are likely to respond to your assertive communication. There is no one 'right' script for a given situation. Instead, we encourage you to see this as an opportunity to practice and experiment with different ways of phrasing what you would like to say. The more you practice, the more you will be able to put these statements into your own words and determine the best script for you, based on the outcomes that you observe.

On a final note here, we also strongly suggest that you first practice your script in front of a mirror or with a friend. This can help you to be sure that your non-verbal communication (e.g., body language) is consistent. You can use Form 9.6 to develop your own assertiveness script for a specific situation.

Situation: _____

My goal: _____

My script:

   1. Empathy statement:_____

   _____

   2. Basic assertion:

      a. I feel _____

      b. when you _____

      c. because_____

   3. State what you would like to change:

      I would like you to_____

   4. Add empathy statement (optional):

      e.g., 'I know this may not have been what you would like to hear . . .'

      _____

      _____

Form 9.6 Assertiveness Script

Other Assertiveness Strategies

Another common situation that requires assertive communication is when someone makes an unfair or unreasonable request or demand. There may also be situations in which the request is reasonable but is simply not something that you would like to do. This can be challenging for individuals who struggle with assertive communication as they may find themselves agreeing to things before they have enough information or agreeing even when they would really like to say no. Table 9.7 includes some strategies to consider when you find yourself in this type of situation.

Monitoring Your Progress

Just like any other time you are learning new skills, the outcome may not be exactly what you hoped for the first time you practice more assertive communication. Keep in mind that changing behavior can be challenging and takes time, patience, and practice. Monitor your efforts as you practice assertive communication over the next weeks and months using Form 9.7. Self-monitoring can help you note what the outcome was in each situation, what worked or did not work as well as you hoped, and what you would like to try to do differently the next time the situation arises. If the outcome is not what you hoped for the first few times, rather than seeing this as a failure on your part, we encourage you to see these as challenging and complex skills that you are in the process of building.

Finally, remember that we can never predict how others respond with perfect accuracy. All we can do is anticipate their response to the best of our ability and alter our communication to be more effective the next time. You may find that, as you develop your assertiveness skills you decide that some relationships that are mainly one-way (i.e., their needs over yours) are not in your best interests to maintain as you prioritize your own health and well-being.

Situation:_____

_____

Time/Date:_____

Outcome:_____

    Advantages:_____

    _____

    Disadvantages:_____

    _____

What I plan to do differently next time (if anything):_____

_____

_____

Form 9.7   Monitoring My Assertiveness Practice

Table 9.7 Strategies for Saying No

Strategies for Saying No

1. If not sure, say you need time to think it over and let the person making a request know when you will have an answer

2. Ask for clarification if you do not fully understand what is requested of you

3. Be as brief as possible and avoid long elaborate explanations and justifications. Such excuses may be used by the other person to argue you out of your 'no'

4. Actually use the word 'no' when declining. 'No' has more power and is less ambiguous than, 'Well, I just don't think so . . .'

5. Make sure your body language and non-verbal gestures are consistent with your verbal message. Shake your head when saying 'no.' Often people unknowingly nod their heads and smile when they are attempting to decline or refuse

6. Use the words 'I won't' or 'I've decided not to,' rather than 'I can't' or 'I shouldn't.' This emphasizes that you have made a choice

7. You may have to decline several times before the person 'hears' you. It is not necessary to come up with a new explanation each time, just repeat your 'no' and your original reason for declining (like a broken record)

8. If the person persists even after you have repeated your 'no' several times, try to change the topic of the conversation. You also have a right to end the conversation

9. Acknowledge feelings involved. 'I know this will be a disappointment to you, but I won't be able to . . .' Remember, you do not need to say, 'I'm sorry.' Apologizing tends to compromise your basic right to say 'no'

10. Remember it is not up to you to solve another person's problems or make that person happy

11. Offer a compromise if you desire, such as, 'I will not be able to babysit for the whole afternoon, but I can sit for 2 hours'

Remember, you can change your mind and say 'no' to a request you originally said 'yes' to. All of the above applies to your change of mind.

Maintaining Your Assertiveness Practice

You now have an idea of several skills and strategies for engaging in assertive communication. The next step is to practice these skills so that they become more familiar and you become more at ease with this type of communication. Our recommendation, as always when changing a complex behavior, is to start small.

If engaging in assertive communication is anxiety provoking for you, a good strategy is to start by practicing these skills in a slightly less anxiety-provoking situation. Practice is an important component here, as in any behavior change. Is there someone you could practice your script with? Try out different ways of expressing what you would like to say so that you feel more comfortable with what you will say. Practicing in front of a mirror or recording yourself with your phone is also an excellent way to check that your non-verbal (behavioral) communication matches what you are saying. The more practice you engage in, the more confident you are likely to feel over time.

Summing It All Up

Assertive communication, involving the direct expression of your needs while acknowledging and respecting the needs of others, is associated with lower levels of distress and better mental health. Learning to communicate assertively takes practice and a planned, strategic approach, including choosing *when* to be assertive and selecting the right person, time, and place for the communication. Planning what you will say in advance in the form of a script can help you stick to your goals during the communication and reduces the chance that you will be 'argued out of' your original position. It is important to practice assertive communication skills and monitor your progress so that you learn from your experience and adapt your approach to ensure that your needs are met.

References

Gjerdingen, D. K., Froberg, D. G., & Fontaine, P. (1991). The effects of social support on women's health during pregnancy, labor and delivery, and the postpartum period. *Family Medicine, 23*, 370–375.

Negron, R., Martin, A., Almog, M., Balbierz, A., & Howell, E. A. (2013). Social support during the postpartum period: Mothers' views on needs, expectations, and mobilization of support. *Maternal and Child Health Journal, 17*, 616–623.

Sarkova, M., Bacikova-Sleskova, M., Orosova, O., Madarasova Geckova, A., Katreniakova, Z., Klein, D., ... Van Dijk, J. P. (2013). Associations between assertiveness, psychological well-being and self-esteem in adolescents. *Journal of Applied Social Psychology, 43*, 147–154.

Segal, D. L. (2005). Relationships of assertiveness, depression and social support among nursing home residents. *Behavior Modification, 29*, 689–695.

Chapter 10

Moving Forward

Maintaining Gains and Managing Slips

How Do I Maintain The Gains I Made Moving Forward?

What Is A Slip Or A Relapse?

What Should I Do If My Symptoms Of Anxiety And Depression Return?

Congratulations! By arriving at this chapter you have learned essential skills and strategies to reduce your anxiety, worry, and depression. One of the main long-term goals of cognitive behavioral therapy (CBT) is to change how you think and behave in order to change how you feel. Treatment gains from CBT last well after treatment ends. In fact, some studies have documented treatment gains up to 10 years following participating in CBT (Durham et al., 2003), which is very encouraging! In order to give yourself the best chance of experiencing *long-term* benefits from the CBT skills and strategies you learned and practiced, it is important that you continue to use these strategies over the next several months. Carving out time for practice and making it a priority can be challenging. Life with a new addition to the family may impose additional demands, so it is easy for you to fall back into 'autopilot,' repeating old (and unhelpful) patterns of thinking and behavior. This can leave you vulnerable to experiencing slips (a temporary return of symptoms), or relapse (a more significant and longer return of symptoms).

Our goal in this chapter is to provide you with some suggestions for maintaining the gains you made in the long term as you move forward. This chapter will also provide you with guidance when you have experienced a slip, namely, when your anxiety or depression has temporarily returned.

First Step: Assess the Gains You Made

Before we can discuss how to maintain your gains in the long term, it is important to examine *what gains* you have made in more detail. Think back to when you just started reading this book. How were you managing your anxiety and depression? How does it compare with how you are feeling these days? What changes have you noticed? There are a number of ways to identify the gains you have made, one of which is quantifying your symptoms of anxiety, worry, or depression on a scale from 0 to 100. As we have stressed in this book, successful treatment of anxiety or depression is not defined as a circumstance in which you no longer experience *any* anxiety or depression. This is because these are normal human experiences and everyone has anxiety and low mood from time to time. We measure gains carefully in a number of ways, including both the severity of your symptoms of anxiety and depression (0 = 'absent or not at all'; 100 = 'debilitating') and the impact they have on your day-to-day functioning (0 = 'not at all interfering'; 100 = 'totally incapacitating').

Using Form 10.1, let's examine the gains you have made with anxiety. Think back to when you started this treatment program and write down several situations that you personally found challenging. Then, under the 'Baseline' heading, rate the severity of your anxiety and how much interference it caused you *before* you started to use the strategies in this book. You may find it helpful to refer back to previous chapters. Next, provide your ratings on how severe and interfering these situations are at the present time under the 'Today' heading.

Situation	Severity 0–100 Not at all – Extremely		Interference 0–100 Not at all – Extremely	
	Baseline	Today	Baseline	Today
Going to the grocery store with my baby (Keesha)	90	55	75	35

Form 10.1 Re-Evaluation of Challenging Situations

In Keesha's example in Form 10.1, notice that she still feels anxious about others' opinions when out in public with her baby. However, the severity of her anxiety in these situations has *decreased* considerably (from severe to moderate) and she is finding that anxiety is much *less* interfering in her day-to-day functioning (from severe to mild). We see this as success as well as a work in progress.

If after completing Form 10.1 your experience is similar and your anxiety is present but not as severe or interfering, then you are certainly on the right track. It is important that you recognize these changes as a result of *your hard work* throughout this program. Remember that change takes time, particularly when you are working on changing habits that may have been present for a long time. Even a small decrease in the severity of symptoms or in their interference is important progress.

Re-Examine Your Goals

Next, think back to the goals you set for yourself at the beginning of this treatment program. Use Form 10.2 to write out your treatment goals and what the outcome is at this point in time. You may want to refer to Chapter 3 to recall your specific goals.

My Goals at The Start of This Program	Outcome
I wanted to stop checking my baby so frequently (Zoë)	*I still check my baby perhaps more than I want to, but the checking has reduced. I also do not feel as anxious in between the times I check*
Develop more of a balance in my life by making time to do more 'me' activities that bring me happiness (Elizabeth)	*I now regularly go for coffee with my friend Sarah every Saturday morning while my husband watches the baby. It's a start!*

Form 10.2 Re-Examination of Goals

Are there any other changes in your day-to-day functioning that you have noticed?

_____

_____

_____

_____

Were any of your goals met either in full or in part? Here, too, we want you to give yourself credit for the progress you have made, even if your goals are not yet fully met. In Zoë's example, you can see that her goal was to reduce her frequency of checking her baby. Although she has indicated that frequent checking is still a challenge for her, she acknowledged that her checking has reduced and she is no longer as anxious in between the times that she checks her baby. In Elizabeth's example, she has started to develop more balance in her day-to-day life by arranging to see her friend Sarah every Saturday morning while her husband watches the baby. She knows this is a step in the right direction and a work in progress.

Next Steps: Maintaining Gains and Moving Forward

Now that you have identified the progress you have made toward your goals in Form 10.2, it is important to develop a plan to maintain these gains in the next months. Further, you may have identified symptoms that have not changed as much as you would like or specific situations that you still find challenging. The next step is to develop a concrete plan to continue your progress and to address the areas that you would like to keep working on. It is important to keep your goals manageable and concrete. You are more likely to make changes if you have a practical step-by-step plan.

Using Form 10.3: (1) write down your plan for maintaining the gains you have made thus far; and (2) write down the next steps to work towards your goals.

Plan for Maintaining Gains	Next Steps with Goals
Continue to practice identifying unhelpful thoughts and develop more helpful thinking in social situations (Keesha)	**My plan:** *Complete a thought-monitoring form once a week with 'new' social situations I am in. Use the best friend technique to generate more helpful thinking*
I won't stew and brew about resentment I feel towards my husband when he does not know what my needs are and I am feeling overwhelmed. I will ensure that I practice open communication and ask for what I need from my husband as the need arises (Elizabeth)	**My plan:** *Go through the assertiveness worksheets to plan what I'll say, starting with an easier situation (e.g., being assertive with my husband). Practice my script with a friend first until I feel comfortable with the message*
1.	**My plan:**
2.	**My plan:**
3.	**My plan:**
4.	**My plan:**

Form 10.3 Plan for Maintaining Gains and New Goals

Notice that Keesha's next steps are concrete and specific. It is not always possible to anticipate when difficult situations will arise. However, many of the challenging situations that we face do tend to recur. Keesha is anticipating that these situations are likely to come up again and is using the skills that she has developed during the program to plan ahead, to lessen the impact of these situations when they occur.

Similarly, Elizabeth is planning to use the assertiveness skills she has developed so she can openly express her needs to her husband at the time she becomes aware of them. This is a work in progress for Elizabeth as she finds it quite difficult to voice her need for balance. She has planned to practice with her friend using a script so she can be more comfortable that the conversation will go as she plans. Planning in advance how you will manage the situations that trigger your symptoms of anxiety and depression is key to maintaining your gains and moving forward. We strongly encourage you to do the same using the tools and exercises in this chapter.

Managing Slips and Relapse

At this point, you will have identified a number of positive changes in both how you feel and what you do and have developed a plan to maintain these gains. However, we know that a slip or temporary return of symptoms can and does occur, even after successfully completing an effective treatment program.

A return of symptoms can occur for a number of different reasons: the occurrence of stressors or challenging situations that you had not anticipated (e.g., loss of your partner's job, costly car repairs needed), biological changes (e.g., hormonal changes), or the increased distress that can come with the experience of simply being a new mother. For example, many women report struggling to manage their anxiety and depression at times when they are exhausted because of interrupted sleep while they are feeding their baby at night. For many women, the competing demands of everyday life and meeting the needs of your baby can lead to feeling overwhelmed and ineffective. Some mothers report an increase in anxiety and worry when they get closer to the time that they plan to return to work and are perhaps thinking (and worrying) about finding chidcare options for their young children.

The experience of the return of symptoms can be unsettling and it is not uncommon to feel like you are 'back at square one.' It is important to remember that setbacks are fairly common. We call these 'slips' because more often than not they are just *temporary* increases in anxiety and depression at times when it is harder to implement your new strategies and skills. Keep in mind that when you are making changes in important areas of your life, change may not occur in a smooth, steady trajectory. You will find that anxiety increases and decreases from time to time. This is a common experience and not necessarily cause for concern, particularly if you are able to engage in the use of your strategies fairly quickly, and see a gradual reduction in your symptoms. In order to better manage slips, consider the steps shown in Figure 10.1.

1. Be Aware

- Be aware of the causes of stress in your life. The more aware you are, the better positioned you are to prepare and take steps to eliminate or minimize stressors and their impact.

2. Distress Management Strategies

- Engage in the distress management strategies learned in this book to reduce distress in the meantime (e.g., more frequent use of paced respiration, going outside, and taking five minutes to yourself).

3. Use Cognitive and Behavior Strategies

- Strategically decide on the cognitive and behavioral strategies that you have learned in this book that are best suited to the situation you are in (e.g., if your baby is crying inconsolably while you are in line at the grocery store you may want to use paced respiration to reduce your own stress while at the same time challenge some of the negative thoughts that you may be having about others judging you negatively).

4. Monitor Your Symptoms

- Continue to monitor your symptoms to be sure that these strategies are helping and that you are gradually feeling better and able to cope.

Figure 10.1 Steps to Manage Slips

What should you do, however, if your symptoms do not seem to be going away or begin to increase substantially over time? A 'relapse' of symptoms is defined as a time when difficulties with functioning and severity of anxiety and depression have fully returned to baseline levels (i.e., where they were when you started the program). Although this can be discouraging, even here it is important to remember that you are not 'back at square one.' You cannot *unlearn* all of the skills, tools, and strategies that you have learned throughout the course of this treatment program. Once you have identified a relapse in anxiety and depression, it is *critical* to build up more support around you, from your family members to your healthcare team, so that you can implement your strategies once again.

The first step in managing a relapse is to identify that it has occurred or that it might occur. Most women can identify a few signs or 'red flags' that symptoms are worsening. Consider the common red flags of relapse shown in Figure 10.2.

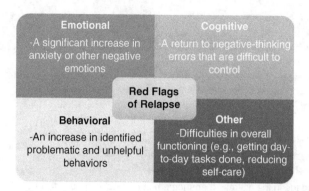

Figure 10.2 Red Flags of Relapse

Using Form 10.4, reflect on and write down what your own 'red flags' are. The more specific you can be, the easier it will be to catch and, ultimately, do something about them.

When I start checking my baby in the middle of the night several times again and it is impacting my sleep, I know that my anxiety is getting worse (Zoë)
When I start to experience thoughts that nothing is going to get better (cognitive) and I stop enjoying my time with my baby, my depression is definitely becoming a problem again (Elizabeth)
1.
2.
3.
4.
5.
6.

Form 10.4   My Red Flags

Keep in mind that identifying any of the 'red flags' in Form 10.4 does not necessarily mean that you are experiencing a *relapse*, but might indicate that this is an increased possibility. The next step is to develop a strategic plan to help you return to your previous level of functioning. By making this 'action plan' in advance (before any of the red flags come about), you will increase the likelihood that you will be able to implement it, if needed, in the future. It will also give you confidence that you have a plan should you need it.

Your action plan (Figure 10.3) should include the following:

1. *Continue to monitor your symptoms and functioning*: As with slips, it is important to be aware of changes in your symptoms and functioning. This also helps you determine whether your action plan for addressing any of the red flags is helping or whether a new plan is needed.

2. *Use those specific cognitive and behavioral strategies you have personally found helpful*: Although strategies might be harder to implement at the moment, it is critical to start to engage in them at this time. Identifying and re-engaging in the use of the tools that you have personally found helpful in this book is strategic. For instance, if you found the use of the 'best friend' technique or the 'examining the evidence' technique effective in the past, it is important to revisit these forms by writing down and walking through your experiences with them. This will give you the best chance of identifying thinking errors and generating more helpful thinking. Also, try reading through the balanced thoughts that you developed in the past. It can be easy to forget these during times of distress and yet they may be particularly important right now.

3. *Continue to engage in self-care activities*: As a new mom, it is very easy to lose sight of the importance of caring for yourself as you may find yourself at the bottom of the priority list. Maintaining your self-care routines, however, is particularly important during times of heightened distress. Examples include showering when your baby is sleeping, dressing for the day, or negotiating for greater support so that you can have time to rest or sleep if possible. These activities

Figure 10.3 Action Plan

may seem small, but can help reduce distress and increase a sense of being able to cope.

4. *Maintain social networks and important relationships*: For new or expecting mothers, the experience of increased fatigue and an increase in daily responsibilities can be overwhelming and can certainly make it difficult to make use of existing social networks. We know, however, that having a good social support network and maintaining close relationships are protective factors when it comes to anxiety and depression.

5. *Seek advice from your healthcare team*: If you notice a change in functioning or worsening of symptoms, we recommend consulting with your family doctor and other relevant members of your health team, including individuals working in perinatal (or general) mental health services. Making sure that these members of your healthcare team are aware of how you feel and how you are functioning is important as it will enable them to provide the best care possible if you experience a worsening of your symptoms.

Considering all of the strategies above, as well as your own personal tried and true strategies, use Form 10.6 (see below) to write down your own action plan. Within the action plan are the steps you will take if you notice that your symptoms start to worsen. Use Zoë's action plan as an example to guide you (Form 10.5).

Zoë's Action Plan to Manage Relapse
1. Talk to my husband and let him know that I started noticing my symptoms again so that he understands how I am feeling and can offer extra support
2. Go back to the 'cognitive' work I did, challenging my anxious thoughts and rereading the more balanced and accurate thoughts I came up with
3. Start with my exposures again, at a challenging but manageable level
4. Ask for extra help with the baby so that I can get more time to sleep as I know how much better I feel when I am less sleep-deprived
5.
6.

Form 10.5 Action Plan: *Zoë's Example*

My Action Plan to Manage Relapse
1.
2.
3.
4.
5.
6.

Form 10.6 Action Plan

Your action plan is critically important for maintaining the gains that you have made throughout this treatment program. Taking the time to complete this now will set up you up for continued gains going forward. This time in your life as you manage all of the changes that come with the new addition to your family is a challenging one. As you have worked through this treatment program, you have developed your approach to managing the stressors that arise and reducing your symptoms of anxiety and depression. You may find that this approach is also useful for times in the future when stress may arise unrelated to your baby.

Summing It All Up

CBT is an effective treatment for anxiety and related symptoms (e.g., worry, depressive symptoms) in new and expecting mothers and the benefits can be seen long after treatment. Change can take time, however, and the best way of maintaining (and continuing) improvements is to continue to use the strategies you have learned in this book in an *intentional* and *strategic* way in the next months. Monitoring your progress over time helps you identify areas that need further change or to be aware of moments when 'slips' have occurred (i.e., temporary worsening of symptoms). This can in turn allow you to respond in a strategic way to minimize the impact on your well-being. A 'relapse' involves a full return of symptoms and difficulties. Having an 'action plan' with steps for you to take is essential, as it can reduce the chance that a full 'relapse' will occur and can help you return more quickly to an optimal level of functioning.

Reference

Durham, R. C., Chambers, J. A., MacDonald, R. R., Power, K. G., & Major, K. (2003). Does cognitive-behavioral therapy influence long-term outcome of generalized anxiety disorder? An 8–14 year follow-up of two clinical trials. *Psychological Medicine, 33,* 499–509. doi:10.1017/S003329170200707

Part III

Other Approaches to Enhance Well-Being

Medication and Support

Chapter 11

Choosing Among the Treatment Options for Anxiety and Depression

Considerations for Medication

What Do I Need to Know About the Use of Medications to Treat Anxiety and Depressive Symptoms in Pregnancy and the Postpartum Period?

What Are the Benefits and Potential Risks of Medications?

What Are Some Other Alternative Treatment Options?

The decision to start a medication during pregnancy or while breastfeeding is a very difficult one. Many factors make this a challenging decision, including feelings of shame, guilt, and worry, and stigma around using medication. Further challenges can include a lack of support from family members and loved ones when deciding to use medication during pregnancy and the postpartum period as well as the financial costs associated with medication. In addition, there is limited scientific evidence about the known and unknown risks for your baby, especially in the long term, which may contribute to you feeling unsure about the decision to use medication.

When considering medication the most important question to ask first is whether medications can decrease anxiety and depression. The answer is yes. Several studies have confirmed that the medications commonly referred to as 'antidepressants' are effective for the treatment of both anxiety and depression. Although these medications are called antidepressants, they are also effective for treatment of anxiety *even when symptoms of depression are not present*. Researchers have faced an important challenge when trying to study the effects of using these medications during pregnancy and when breastfeeding on both mothers and their babies as most of the research has been limited to studying women who became pregnant while already using antidepressants or women who chose to start medication during their pregnancy (Payne, 2017; Stewart & Vigod, 2016). Below we will discuss the alternative treatment options that have been shown to reduce anxiety and depressive symptoms in pregnancy and the postpartum period.

Medications in Pregnancy and When Breastfeeding

When Does It Makes Sense to Use Antidepressants?

The decision to *start* an antidepressant medication during pregnancy or the post-partum period is not exactly the same as the decision to *remain* on medication while you are pregnant or breastfeeding. Women who are doing well on an antidepressant medication and who would like to consider stopping the medication *before* becoming pregnant or at the beginning of their pregnancy should ideally wean themselves off the medication under the close supervision of a physician. Medications need to be discontinued slowly in order that possible early worsening of anxiety and depressive symptoms when stopping the medication can be monitored.

For those women who are leaning towards discontinuing antidepressant medication *during* pregnancy, it is important to consider what has happened when previous attempts were made to stop medication (Figure 11.1).

These questions are critically important to consider and discuss with your healthcare professional. Another important question is whether the medication you are using is considered safe or unsafe during pregnancy (see below). If your anxiety has significantly worsened when you have previously attempted to discontinue medication, you may choose to continue the medication during pregnancy. There is evidence that previous anxiety increases the risk for re-experiencing anxiety during the perinatal period so for some women the option to maintain the medication is reasonable, as long as the potential risks are fully discussed and understood (see below).

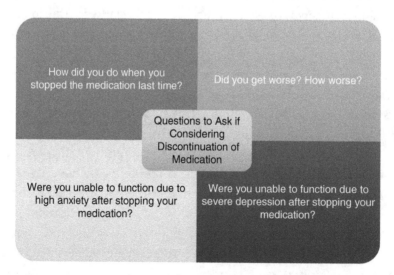

Figure 11.1 Questions to Ask if Considering Discontinuing Medication

For women who experience anxiety during pregnancy or the postpartum period and who wish to consider starting a medication, important questions to consider include those given in Figure 11.2.

While studies that investigate medications for *anxiety* during pregnancy and while breastfeeding are largely lacking, we refer to the guidelines on pharmacological treatment for perinatal depression (MacQueen et al., 2016; Payne, 2017; Stewart & Vigod, 2016). The reasons are: (1) the medications recommended for anxiety and depression are the same (antidepressants); (2) anxiety and depression can be equally distressing and disabling; and (3) anxiety and depression often co-occur. If you are experiencing mild to moderate anxiety, medications are not recommended as a first-line treatment choice. At this severity level, the first-line treatment choice would be a non-pharmacological treatment such as cognitive behavioral therapy (CBT) (Williams et al., 2014). However, in cases of moderate to severe anxiety where non-pharmacological treatments were *not* effective, and/or the level of maternal distress is incapacitating, medication options should be considered (MacQueen et al., 2016).

Most treatment guidelines recommend selective serotonin reuptake inhibitors (SSRIs) and serotonin and norepinephrine reuptake inhibitors (SNRIs) as first-line agents for treatment of anxiety disorders (Bandelow et al., 2015; Katzman et al., 2014). These medications increase substances called serotonin and norepinephrine in the brain and lead to a reduction in anxiety and depressive symptoms. However, as we noted above, researchers are not able to fully study these medications in pregnancy and postpartum using a study design that would properly reveal their benefits and risks because it is considered unethical to randomize (or unbiasedly locate) mothers to receive medication or a placebo (sugar pill). The best safety information we have regarding the use of these medications in pregnancy and during breastfeeding comes from large observational or population databases (Grzeskowiak et al., 2016; Malm et al., 2015; Wisner et al., 2009).

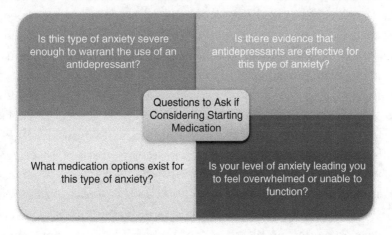

Figure 11.2   Questions to Ask if Considering Starting Medication

As outlined in the latest clinical guidelines published in 2016 by the Canadian Network for Mood and Anxiety Treatments (MacQueen et al., 2016), we also recommend the SSRIs, including citalopram (Celexa), escitalopram (Cipralex), or sertraline (Zoloft) as reasonable options when medications are indicated in pregnancy or during breastfeeding. Other options include the SNRIs venlafaxine (Effexor) or duloxetine (Cymbalta). Fluoxetine (Prozac) and paroxetine (Paxil) may be options during breastfeeding but we *would not* recommend these medications during pregnancy due to the risks noted below.

Special Considerations during Pregnancy

The following risks should be considered when deciding to use antidepressant medication during pregnancy: (1) birth defects; (2) obstetric and neonatal outcomes; and (3) long-term health effects in the baby.

Risk of Birth Defects

In general, most studies do not associate SSRIs or SNRIs with a significant risk of birth defects, with perhaps the exemption of paroxetine (Paxil) and fluoxetine (Prozac). Paroxetine has been associated with a specific risk of heart defect in the baby, but later studies questioned this association. Given that the evidence is not clear on the risk of heart defects with paroxetine and the small risk for birth defects associated with the use of fluoxetine, we do not recommend the use of either of these medications during the first trimester of pregnancy. To date, the other SSRIs and SNRIs have not been associated with increased risk of birth defects.

Obstetric and Neonatal Outcomes

SSRIs and SNRIs have been associated with a small increased risk of a number of negative outcomes, including spontaneous abortions, preterm delivery, and poorer physical health in newly delivered babies. However, many of these studies did not separate out the risks of the medications and the risks of the mother's mental illness. The studies that did account for severity of mother's mental distress found that both antidepressant medication and maternal depression and anxiety carry similar risks for most of these negative outcomes.

One exemption is the so-called 'poor neonatal adaptation syndrome' (PNAS), which has a well-established risk that affects 15–30% of babies exposed to antidepressants in the third trimester of pregnancy. Symptoms of PNAS may include jitteriness, irritability, tremor, respiratory distress, excessive crying, difficulty feeding, and difficulty sleeping. In the vast majority of cases, these symptoms are mild and short-lived, resolving in 2–14 days. Importantly, this syndrome is *not* associated with increased mortality and is *not* associated with long-term developmental problems in the baby. There is some evidence that

PNAS may be more common with the use of fluoxetine, paroxetine, and venlafaxine.

Finally, exposure to antidepressants in the third trimester of gestation has been associated with a small increased risk of persistent pulmonary hypertension in the baby (3–3.5 cases per 1,000 infants, compared to 2 cases per 1,000 infants in the general population).

Long-Term Developmental Consequences for Babies

The majority of available studies have not found an association between use of antidepressants in pregnancy and long-term negative consequences on the baby's emotional, cognitive, or motor development. Interestingly, studies do show that the severity of a mother's distress was an important factor predicting later emotional and physical performance in children (Gentile, 2017; Grzeskowiak et al., 2016; Rotem-Kohavi & Oberlander, 2017). The recent association with an increase in autism spectrum disorders with the use of antidepressant medication during pregnancy is still unresolved. There are as many studies suggesting a positive association as there are suggesting a negative association. Of note is that the major criticism of these studies is, in fact, the inability to account for the severity of maternal distress (depression, anxiety, stress; Andrade, 2017; Morales et al., 2018).

Special Considerations during the Postpartum Period

Studies suggest that between 45% and 75% of the maternal dosage of an antidepressant is transferred to the fetus through the placenta (Ewing et al., 2015). However, antidepressants are secreted at much lower levels in breast milk (Kronenfeld et al., 2017). In the case of SSRIs and SNRIs, less than 10% of the maternal dosage of an antidepressant is typically detected in the breast milk, with sertraline and paroxetine having particularly low relative infant dosages (0.5–3%; Newton & Hale, 2015). While there have been isolated case reports in the literature describing adverse events in infants exposed to antidepressants through breast milk, these events are uncommon and, when they happen, they are typically mild and short-lived (Kronenfeld et al., 2017).

Reliable Online Resources

Given that the literature on the safety of medication use in pregnancy and breastfeeding is constantly evolving, the following websites are recommended for you to access so you can keep yourself updated on the latest developments in this area:

American College of Obstetricians and Gynecologists (U.S.) www.acog.org/Patients/FAQs/Postpartum-Depression

Canadian Paediatric Society Position Statement www.cps.ca/en/documents/posi
tion/SSRI-infant-outcomes

MGH Center for Women's Mental Health https://womensmentalhealth.org/

Motherisk www.motherisk.org/ (free helpline: 1-877-439-2744)

Alternative Treatments

A number of other treatments have been tested to reduce anxiety and depression
during pregnancy and the postpartum period. Perhaps one of the most promising
results came from a 6-week group intervention conducted in pregnant women who
were depressed or anxious, or were considered at high risk for developing anxiety and
depression (Thomas et al., 2014). This program included behavioral self-care
strategies, psychoeducation, interpersonal therapy, and parent–infant relationship.
They found improvement in anxiety and depressive symptoms, as well as maternal
attachment (Thomas et al., 2014).

Multiple clinical trials have tested yoga as an alternative treatment for anxiety in
pregnancy and the postpartum period. While some studies found that yoga alle-
viated anxiety symptoms in women with mild anxiety or depressive symptoms
(Buttner et al., 2015; Newham et al., 2014; Satyapriya et al., 2013), the only
study that tested yoga in women with a *clinical diagnosis* of anxiety or depressive
disorder found no improvement in anxiety or depressive symptoms (Davis et al.,
2015). As such, although yoga might be a useful option for healthy women with
mild anxiety or depressive symptoms, this method of treatment would likely not be
effective in women whose anxiety or depressive symptoms are severe enough to
interfere with their ability to function. In addition, there is no evidence that yoga is
helpful in the long run. Lastly, studies investigating mindfulness meditation, and
relaxation techniques did not find that these activities significantly improved anxiety
symptoms in pregnant mothers.

Summing It All Up

Some medications, particularly the SSRIs or SNRIs, may be useful in the treatment
of moderate to severe anxiety in pregnancy and the postpartum period. The potential
risks and benefits of medication use should be fully discussed with your healthcare
provider for a better-informed decision. We encourage you to include your partner
and/or key family members in the discussion so that they can support your decision.
Research on the potential risks related to the use of medications in pregnancy and
the postpartum period is constantly being updated; therefore, we encourage you to
seek advice from specialists and look up information from reliable resources,
including the ones provided in this chapter. There are effective alternatives to
medication that should also be considered, with the first-line choice being CBT (as
outlined in this book).

References

Andrade, C. (2017). Antidepressant exposure during pregnancy and risk of autism in the offspring, 1: Meta-review of meta-analysis. *Journal of Clinical Psychiatry*, 78(8), e1047–e1051.

Bandelow, B., Lichte, T., Rudolf, S., Wiltink, J., & Beutel, M. E. (2015). The German guidelines for the treatment of anxiety disorders. *European Archives of Psychiatry: Clinical Neuroscience*, 265, 363–373.

Buttner, M. M., Brock, R. L., O'Hara, M. W., & Stuart, S. (2015). Efficacy of yoga for depressed postpartum women: A randomized controlled trial. *Complementary Therapies in Clinical Practice*, 21(2), 94–100.

Davis, K., Goodman, S. H., Leiferman, J., Taylor, M., & Dimidjian, S. (2015). A randomized controlled trial of yoga for pregnant women with symptoms of depression and anxiety. *Complementary Therapies in Clinical Practice*, 21(3), 166–172.

Ewing, G., Tatarchuk, Y., Appleby, D., Schwartz, N., & Kim, D. (2015). Placental transfer of antidepressant medications: Implications for postnatal adaptation syndrome. *Clinical Pharmacokinetics*, 54(4), 359–370.

Gentile, S. (2017). Untreated depression during pregnancy: Short-and long-term effects in offspring. A systematic review. *Neuroscience*, 342, 154–166.

Grzeskowiak, L. E., Morrison, J. L., Henriksen, T. B., Bech, B. H., Obel, C., Olsen, J., & Pedersen, L. H. (2016). Prenatal antidepressant exposure and child behavioral outcomes at 7 years of age: A study within the Danish National Birth Cohort. *British Journal of Obstetrics and Gynaecology*, 123, 1919–1928.

Katzman, M. A., Bleau, P., Blier, P., Chokka, P., Kjernisted, K., & Van Ameringen, M. (2014). Canadian guidelines for the management of anxiety, posttraumatic stress and obsessive-compulsive disorders. *BMC Psychiatry*, 14, S1. doi:10.1186/1471-244x-14-s1-s1.

Kronenfeld, N., Berlin, M., Shaniv, D., & Berkovitch, M. (2017). Use of psychotropic medications in breastfeeding women. *Birth Defects Research*, 109(12), 957–997.

MacQueen, G. M., Frey, B. N., Ismail, Z., Jaworska, N., Steiner, M., Lieshout, R. J., & Ravindran, A. V. (2016). Depression work group. Canadian Network for Mood and Anxiety Treatments (CANMAT). Clinical guidelines for the management of adults with major depressive disorder: Section 6. Special populations: Youth, women, and the elderly. *Canadian Journal of Psychiatry*, 61, 588–603.

Malm, H., Sourander, A., Gissler, M., Gyllenberg, D., Hinkka-Yli-Salomäki, S., McKeague, I. W., & Brown, A. S. (2015). Pregnancy complications following prenatal exposure to SSRIs or maternal psychiatric disorders: Results from population-based national register data. *American Journal of Psychiatry*, 172, 1224–1232.

Morales, D. R., Slattery, J., Evans, S., & Kurz, X. (2018). Antidepressant use during pregnancy and risk of autism spectrum disorder and attention deficit hyperactivity disorder: Systematic review of observational studies and methodological considerations. *BMC Medicine*, 16(1), 6.

Newham, J. J., Wittkowski, A., Hurley, J., Aplin, J. D., & Westwood, M. (2014). Effects of antenatal yoga on maternal anxiety and depression: A randomized controlled trial. *Depression and Anxiety*, 31(8), 631–640.

Newton, E. R., & Hale, T. W. (2015). Drugs in breast milk. *Clinical Obstetrics and Gynecology*, 58(4), 868–884.

Payne, J. L. (2017). Psychopharmacology in pregnancy and breastfeeding. *Psychiatric Clinics of North America*, 40, 217–238.

Rotem-Kohavi, N., & Oberlander, T. F. (2017). Variations in neurodevelopmental outcomes in children with prenatal SSRI antidepressant exposure. *Birth Defects Research*, 109(12), 909–923.

Satyapriya, M., Nagarathna, R., Padmalatha, V., & Nagendra, H. R. (2013). Effect of integrated yoga on anxiety, depression and well-being in normal pregnancy. *Complementary Therapies in Clinical Practice*, 19(4), 230–236.

Stewart, D. E., & Vigod, S. (2016). Postpartum depression. *New England Journal of Medicine*, *375*, 2177–2186.

Thomas, N., Komiti, A., & Judd, F. (2014). Pilot early intervention antenatal group program for pregnant women with anxiety and depression. *Archives of Women's Mental Health*, *17*, 503–509.

Williams, J., Ryan, D., Thomas-Peter, K., Walker, J., Cadario, B., & Li, D. (2014). *Best practice guidelines for mental health disorders in the perinatal period*. BC Reproductive Mental Health Program & Perinatal Services BC. Retrieved from: www.perinatalservicesbc.ca/ Documents/Guidelines-Standards/Maternal

Wisner, K. L., Sit, D. K., Hanusa, B. H., Moses-Kolko, E. L., Bogen, D. L., Hunker, D. F., & Singer, L. T. (2009). Major depression and antidepressant treatment: Impact on pregnancy and neonatal outcomes. *American Journal of Psychiatry*, *166*, 557–566.

Chapter 12

Strengthening Your Support Network to Reduce Stress

How Do I Speak to My Family and Loved Ones About My Anxiety and Depression?
How Can My Family and Loved Ones Help Me? How Do I Ask?
How Can I Help My Loved One During Her Pregnancy and Postpartum?

Until this point, the focus of this book has been on the challenges you may face with anxiety and depression during pregnancy or the post-partum period (i.e., the 'perinatal period'). The material covered thus far has helped you develop: (1) a greater awareness of your anxiety, depression, or related symptoms; (2) a better understanding of *why* these symptoms often increase during the perinatal period, even if you were not particularly anxious or depressed prior to pregnancy; and (3) tools that you can use to reduce and better manage your symptoms of anxiety and/or depression. We know, however, that your experience during the perinatal period may also affect people around you. Families and other members of your social support network play an important role in helping you reduce your emotional distress during this time. Building and maintaining a strong support network is critical as women who report feelings of isolation in the perinatal period are at greater risk for worsening of anxiety and depression symptoms (Dennis & Ross, 2006; Figueiredo et al., 2008).

A social support network typically includes your partner as well as your parents and in-laws, siblings, friends, extended family members (e.g., cousins, aunts), and resources in the community. Unfortunately, one of the most common sources of distress that women report is perceived lack of support, particularly in the first weeks or months after delivery (Dennis & Ross, 2006). This is true for women in general during pregnancy and the postpartum period but it is *particularly true* for women who are struggling with anxiety or depression. Often times this may be a result of family members living far away, lack of local community services, your own personal challenges in seeking/accepting help (e.g., anxiety about asking for help when help is needed), or in some cases a lack of available support (e.g., living in a city far from family or a recent move away from people you are close to). In addition, people who are a part of your social support network can struggle with knowing just *how* to help. The first part of this chapter focuses on how to maximize your personal social supports. The last part of the chapter is for you to share with those to whom you are close so they can know how best to support you during this time.

Making the Most of Your Support Network

We have found that family members and loved ones who make up your support network often *want* to provide help and support but may lack the information they need to offer this help in an effective manner. The following strategies can be helpful in rallying and strengthening your support networks.

Information

Educate loved ones with information about the nature of anxiety and depressive symptoms that can arise during the perinatal period.

We suggest planning a time when you can sit down and discuss this information calmly together. Having this discussion in a hurry or when everyone is tired or under stress may not be the best time. We also strongly encourage you to review parts of the cognitive behavioral therapy (CBT) program materials in this book with members of your support network. This chapter also contains a section with reading material that loved ones may find helpful (see below).

Planning

Plan ahead to maximize support. Women most often report that they lack what we call *instrumental support*; that is, help with managing day-to-day tasks such as taking care of the household (e.g., laundry, washing dishes) and childcare.

Having a clear idea of what support you need *before* sitting down to talk can help your loved ones have a better idea of how they can help. Try to be *as specific as possible* when identifying areas where help is needed. For example, asking a partner to 'be a better partner' is generally not helpful (where does your partner start?). Instead, we suggest identifying specific areas in your day-to-day life where you feel overwhelmed and could use a hand. An expectation that the loved one will 'know or guess' how to help may generate frustration and interpersonal conflict, which can be avoided with good communication.

Work through the problem-solving section of this workbook – on your own and with your loved one – to identify specific, concrete goals or tasks that your loved one or other member of your support network may be able to help you with (e.g., meal preparation, specific household tasks, childcare while you take some time for yourself).

Battle Barriers in Asking for Help

Challenge thoughts that might be getting in the way of asking for help.

It is not uncommon for women to express concern about asking for help. You may express the belief, for example, that in order to be a good mother you *must* be able to manage *all* of the demands and uncertainties of raising children on your own with absolute ease and confidence. If such a person exists, we have not met her! Raising children and maintaining a family can be wonderfully satisfying *but at the same time* exhausting and challenging. Rallying your support network is a reasonable goal to make the many demands on your time and energy more manageable. This is true for women experiencing anxiety or depression.

The following are some common unhelpful thoughts about asking for help that we have encountered among the women we work with:

- 'If I ask for help, others will think I'm a failure as a mother.'

- 'Other women seem to be able to manage all of this without a problem – I should be able to as well.'

- 'If I'm not the one taking care of everything, it won't be done right! I can't risk delegating anything.'

If these thoughts are familiar to you, review the strategies that you learned earlier in this book for (1) identifying thinking errors and unhelpful thoughts and (2) generating more balanced thinking (Chapters 4 and 5). The list of questions to challenge unhelpful thinking can be useful here as well (e.g., what evidence do you have that other mothers are managing without *any* difficulties? Are there any mothers that you know who you think are great mothers *and* who sometimes struggle?).

Use assertive communication skills to maximize the likelihood that you receive the support you need. We strongly encourage you to apply the assertiveness skills that you learned earlier in this book (see Chapter 9) when asking others for help or support, particularly if previous efforts did not lead to the help you needed. Using assertive communication can increase the chance that (1) you will be asking for help that will meet your specific needs and (2) that the person you are speaking to will respond as you hoped. We cannot force others to change. However, we can communicate in a way that increases the likelihood that we will obtain the help we need.

Acknowledge Others' Feelings and Experience

Acknowledge any distress your partner or other important members of your support network may be feeling.

The perinatal period is not only a time of tremendous change for you as an expecting or new mother, but also for new or expecting partners and other important members of your support network. In fact, there is a small but important correlation between stress, anxiety, and depression in new and expecting mothers and the presence of these same symptoms in their partners (Goodman, 2004; Matthey et al., 2003).

Unfortunately, the distress experienced by new or expecting partners or other members of support networks often goes unaddressed. Partners often struggle with many of the same concerns as new or expecting mothers (e.g., worry about being a good parent or partner, changes in identity, changes in the nature of the romantic relationship with you, anxiety about supporting a growing family financially). Moreover, surveys show that partners of women who are anxious or depressed sometimes choose not to disclose their own concerns for fear of further 'burdening' their partners (Fonseca & Canavarro, 2017; Rowe et al., 2013).

Asking your partner about any stress, anxiety, or depression that he/she may be experiencing can help your partner feel supported and often opens the door to a broader discussion about working on parenting and other responsibilities as a team. If your partner is anxious or experiencing depression, we suggest that he/she too might benefit from some of the resources and strategies in this book. Alternatively, encouraging your partner to seek help through the family physician or other community healthcare services may help to address his or her concerns and, ultimately, help your partner to be as supportive as possible for you.

Seeking Support from Other Places

Seek other sources of support.

Not everyone has a close social network available to help. However, community resources often exist but may be sometimes hard to find. We suggest seeking out information about additional sources of support in the following ways:

- Speak with your family doctor about resources for new parents or for adults dealing with mental health difficulties in the community.

- Seek out government-funded or subsidized programs that offer a number of social and instrumental support services for new and expecting mothers and their families (e.g., discussion or peer support groups, play centers for children, services with a registered nurse on site, educational and physical exercise activities). These can be invaluable for the support services that they offer but can also offer an opportunity for you to meet other women with similar concerns. This, in turn, can help you feel less isolated by building a social network and allow you to learn of other opportunities available for support services in your community.

- Speak with other mothers in your area, members of your family who have small children, or join online groups for mothers struggling with similar concerns. These can be useful sources of information about services or support networks in your area.

■ Consider joining a mom-and-baby activity group in your community (e.g., yoga, walking, play group). This will help you develop links with women who are facing similar challenges who may be able to understand what you are going through in ways that others in your life may not.

Help Your Support System Know How to Help You

For many women, those around them may not know how to reach out and provide support. Share the reading below with your partner or close loved ones from whom you would like to get more support. Increasing their knowledge will empower them to better support you during this challenging time in your life.

How Can I Help? Reading for Loved Ones

Understanding the Nature of Anxiety and Depression During Pregnancy and Postpartum Period

The perinatal period (i.e., pregnancy and up to 1 year postpartum) can be a period of considerable joy and excitement for families. This period can also be associated with considerable changes and challenges for new and expecting mothers and their families. Some mothers may face physical (e.g., discomfort or reduced mobility in pregnancy, fatigue and recovery in the postpartum), emotional (e.g., increased stress, anxiety, worry, or depression), psychological (e.g., challenges adjusting to new roles in the family), social (e.g., changes in the primary focus of the romantic relationship or friendships), and financial challenges (e.g., increased costs associated with having a new baby), just to name a few. In addition, women also undergo intense (however normal) hormonal changes, including elevation of specific hormones (e.g., estrogen, progesterone), especially during late pregnancy and early postpartum. Estrogen in particular plays an important role in the brain's ability to regulate emotion.

Given the many changes that women undergo during the perinatal period, it is perhaps not surprising that stress, anxiety, and depressive symptoms can increase during this time. Women often report, for example, an increase in feelings of sadness or irritability, particularly in the weeks just after childbirth (often referred to as the 'baby blues' in the first few weeks after delivery). In addition to depression, recent research shows that symptoms of anxiety are *at least as common, if not more so,* than symptoms of depression during pregnancy and postpartum. For the most part, a mild increase in anxiety or depressive symptoms over the course of pregnancy or in the early postpartum period is considered to be *normal*. For many women, these symptoms begin to decrease in the months after delivery. For some women, these symptoms can involve worsening of pre-existing difficulties with anxiety or depressive symptoms. For other women, these symptoms may be new and may be particularly upsetting if they have not struggled with them before. Whatever the source, anxiety and depression can increase to the point of significant interference in daily functioning. Being able to identify the symptoms of anxiety and depression can help partners and loved ones better understand when treatment or additional support may be warranted.

Common Signs of Anxiety

Signs of heightened anxiety can include increased *avoidance* of situations that may trigger anxiety (e.g., going to the grocery store, visiting with friends), thoughts that show a strong bias toward negative outcomes, often referred to as worst-case scenario or catastrophic thinking (e.g., 'when I am at the grocery store the baby will cry uncontrollably and I won't be able to soothe him'), or behaviors that might reduce anxiety in the short term but tend to maintain it in the longer term. These behaviors can include excessive and repeated reassurance seeking, repeated checking (e.g., repeatedly calling to check that a family member is safe), or repeating actions over and over again (e.g., rewashing baby bottles to make sure they are sterile). It should be noted that any of these behaviors can be helpful for most of us some of the time. If done excessively, however, they may actually *reduce* rather than increase a person's confidence and may maintain rather than reduce anxiety in the long term.

Common Signs of Depression

When we talk about 'depression' in a clinical context we are generally referring to the symptoms associated with major depressive disorder (MDD). This is a diagnosable mental health condition that is primarily characterized by feeling sad, down, or depressed. Another common experience is the loss of interest or pleasure in the things that a person would normally enjoy (e.g., a favorite meal, social interactions, hobbies). Additional symptoms must also be present and can include an increase or decrease in appetite, increased or decreased sleep, extreme fatigue, problems with concentration, feelings of worthlessness or excessive guilt, and thoughts of suicide.

Aside from thoughts of suicide, we may all experience some of these symptoms from time to time. A clinical diagnosis is only given if these symptoms are present for most of the day, nearly every day, for a minimum of 2 weeks. These symptoms must also be associated with significant emotional distress and/or interfere with daily functioning to warrant a diagnosis of MDD or 'clinical depression.' Finally, these symptoms must be present to a greater degree than what would be expected under the circumstances (e.g., greater fatigue than would be expected given that new mothers are often waking repeatedly at night to feed their baby). Examples of impaired functioning can include difficulties completing daily or routine tasks such as household care, self-care (e.g., not getting out of bed, not dressing or showering) and withdrawal from social or other important responsibilities.

Treatment for Anxiety and Depression During the Pregnancy and the Postpartum

A variety of treatments have been developed and are effective in treating anxiety and depression among women in the perinatal period. Medications commonly referred to as *antidepressants* can influence how we feel and how we think. They have been shown to be effective for women with anxiety or depression during both pregnancy and the postpartum period. More information on medications used in the treatment of anxiety and depression in the perinatal period can be found in Chapter 11. In our clinical practice, however, some women are advised not to take medication at specific times in their pregnancy. Other women simply choose not to use antidepressants for a variety of reasons, including concerns about side effects or potential risks associated with medication use.

In addition, we have found that women who are taking medication during pregnancy and the postpartum period only partly benefit and continue to experience symptoms that interfere with daily functioning despite regular use of medications. For these women, a combination of medication and non-pharmacological treatment options is ideal. It is for these reasons that non-pharmacological, therapy-based treatments are increasingly recommended for women with anxiety or depression during the perinatal period either as an alternative to or in conjunction with medication.

CBT is the first-line psychological treatment for anxiety and depressive disorders in adults. Research evidence has accumulated over the past four decades supporting the effectiveness of this treatment (Butler et al., 2006; Chambless & Ollendick, 2001). Further, several recent studies support the effectiveness of CBT for anxiety and depression in women during the perinatal period, including reductions in anxiety, worry, and depressive symptoms following treatment (Green et al., 2015; Marchesi et al., 2016; Stephens et al., 2016). CBT is a practical, skills-based treatment in which women start by learning more about the nature of anxiety and depressive symptoms during pregnancy and the postpartum period. CBT is based on the idea that how we think in a given situation has a strong influence on the emotions we feel in that situation and on how we behave or respond. We know that individuals with long-term anxiety and depression tend to show specific patterns in their thinking that may not be helpful and may lead to behaviors that can contribute to the distress. In individuals with long-term anxiety, for instance, we often see 'catastrophic' or worst-case scenario thinking (e.g., 'My partner is late coming home from work – he must have been in a terrible accident'). In individuals with depression, we often see thinking that is negative about the self (e.g., 'I am not worth it,' 'I can't do anything right'), about others (e.g., 'Others will be critical or judging'), and about the future (e.g., 'There is no hope, nothing will change').

In CBT programs for anxiety and depression, individuals learn strategies to identify when specific thoughts may be unhelpful and add to their distress.

Individuals then learn strategies to challenge unhelpful thinking and to generate more balanced thinking as well as strategies to develop more helpful behavioral responses. For example, for an individual who repeatedly fears that her partner has been in a fatal accident if the person is late coming home from work, we might start by identifying the specific thoughts that may be adding to this distress (e.g., 'Serious accidents happen every day' or 'I need to be sure he is safe or I won't be able to cope'). Individuals are then given strategies to help generate more balanced thinking (e.g., examining past evidence that either supports or challenges the anxious thought). Note that by 'more balanced thinking' we do not mean unrealistically positive thinking (e.g., 'he will never be in a car accident') or empty reassurance (e. g., 'everything will be fine'). Instead, balanced thinking acknowledges any basis for the worries while also taking into consideration information that might counter the anxious prediction (e.g., 'Although accidents do happen in the area where my husband drives, he is generally an excellent driver. He has only ever been in one accident several years ago and it was a minor fender-bender'). Finally, we work to identify behaviors that may be unhelpful (e.g., repeated calls to ensure partner's safety) and develop a plan for gradually reducing these behaviors over time.

In this book, an approach called behavioral activation is also recommended for individuals with depression (Chapter 8). This approach fits under the broad umbrella of CBT strategies for depression. Behavioral activation is based on the idea that we tend to withdraw from pleasurable or satisfying activities when feeling down or depressed. Although this may be understandable given the fatigue and loss of pleasure that can be experienced with depression, we also know that this tendency to withdraw can maintain or even increase symptoms over time because we no longer get the enjoyable feelings associated with them. In this approach, individuals are encouraged to gradually and strategically add activities back in their days that might have given them at least some sense of pleasure or satisfaction in the past.

Supporting Your Loved One During Her Pregnancy or Postpartum Period

Seeing your loved one struggle with anxiety or depression during pregnancy or the postpartum period can be an unsettling and anxiety-provoking experience for members of a woman's support network. In our clinical practice, we often have partners or other members of the support network tell us that they would like to help, but are not sure *how*. The following are some suggestions for providing support to a loved one who is struggling with anxiety or depression during her pregnancy or in the postpartum period.

Showing Interest

Show your interest in learning more about her experiences with anxiety or depression as well as other challenges she may be facing. Ask for information on perinatal anxiety or depression or ask if your loved one is comfortable with you reviewing parts, or all, of this book. We have found that women who sit down to go through some of the material about CBT and the nature of perinatal anxiety and depression with their partners or family members often report feeling more supported and better able to identify the specific areas where they need help.

If she is attending a physician's appointment where issues related to anxiety or depression might be brought up, you might ask if she would be comfortable with you attending the appointment in order to better understand as well as get more information on ways in which you can provide support.

Remember, just showing your interest in understanding her experience can open the door to more open and honest communication about the distress or difficulties that you may both be experiencing.

Communication

Work at maintaining open communication (and showing your interest) about challenges that arise. Good communication can go a long way towards helping a woman who is struggling with perinatal anxiety or depression to feel understood and to feel hopeful that you will be able to work together as a team when resolving challenges or accessing services that are needed.

Family members or other members of the support network can sometimes hesitate to ask directly about how a woman is coping in the perinatal period. However, we have found that asking in a non-accusatory manner can be a source of relief and lead to more honest communication.

The women we work with sometimes tell us that they hesitate to open up about their anxiety or depression because they do not wish to burden their partners with their concerns. Opening a helpful/supportive line of communication might start with questions that reflect what you have observed (e.g., 'I have noticed that you seem more overwhelmed these days, is that right? If so, can you tell me a bit more about how this is going for you and how I might be able to help?')

Finally, keep in mind that someone who is anxious or depressed may not be ready to discuss thoughts or feelings that are painful. However, knowing that the offer of supportive listening is available when she is ready can in itself help reduce her distress.

Offer to Help

Offer to help but be open to negotiating the nature and timing of help.

Keep in mind that someone who is anxious or feeling depressed may not know exactly what would be most helpful. Offering to simply listen or to sit down and help problem solve around specific concerns may help her identify the nature of help that would be most appreciated.

Some of the most common areas to help include:

- helping out with housework (or considering hiring a cleaning service if that is financially viable)

- helping out with meal preparation or shopping

- helping out with the baby at night so your partner can get some sleep or offering to take the baby early in the morning so your partner can sleep in

- suggesting that your partner plan some time each week to take for herself and you will take the baby. She may really appreciate going out on her own or she may prefer to have some alone time in the house.

Support Balance in Her Life

Provide support in her efforts to maintain pleasurable or enjoyable activities. Individuals who are depressed tend to withdraw from specific activities (e.g., social activities, hobbies, physical exercise). This can increase social isolation and exacerbate symptoms of depression.

We suggest trying to provide support by encouraging your loved one to add in small, manageable activities that are enjoyable on a daily basis. Activities that can be particularly important include spending time with friends or other members of a woman's social network, and gradually increasing exercise is a good start. Remember that it is important to add these activities in a way that is *manageable* given her current level of energy and the demands on her time. For instance, going from no exercise to exercising four to five times per week may not be a reasonable goal but adding one or two 20-minute walks with you in the evenings with the family might be more manageable.

Understanding Anxious and Depressed Thoughts

Provide support in her efforts to challenge unhelpful thinking. First, let us just say that a CBT approach is *not* about the idea that most of what a woman thinks is incorrect or that all of her efforts to reduce her anxiety are problematic. In fact, the worries or anxiety that women express do generally have a basis in their direct experiences or are consistent with what we know to be true statistically (i.e., bad things can and do happen and we do need to be prepared). Indeed, women in the perinatal period generally have a good understanding of the areas where they need to be concerned and many of the things that will help reduce distress. Having said that, we often see that individuals who experience long-term and consuming anxiety have a tendency to think in worst-case scenario or 'catastrophic' ways and to engage in behaviors that may maintain anxiety in the longer term (e.g., excessive reassurance seeking, repeated checking, and avoidance).

If your loved one is working on reducing these unhelpful behaviors, we suggest having an open conversation about what her goals are and asking how you might be able to support her in this process. For instance, if your loved one knows that she tends to ask repeatedly for reassurance and yet this reassurance is not having the desired effect of reducing her anxiety, you may work together to find a more helpful response than simple reassurance. In fact, we find that simple reassurance (e.g., 'It will all be fine') is not effective in reducing anxiety. Similarly, dismissing worries or anxiety (e.g., 'You don't need to worry – stop worrying about this!') tends not to reduce worry either (most of us are not able to simply stop emotions on command).

Instead, we suggest helping to generate more balanced thinking and to encourage a reduction in excessive reassurance by asking questions that support a more balanced point of view. Examples include:

> I guess we don't really know how this will turn out. However, while it's possible it could go badly, how likely is that? How often has it gone badly before? When it has gone badly in the past, just how bad was it? Were you (or were we) able to problem solve around this type of situation before? If so, is it possible that we might be able to do so again?

Appreciate When It Is Time for Her to Get Help

Help to identify additional resources and treatment when needed.

If you notice signs that your loved one seems to be experiencing an increase in anxiety or depression, we suggest that you speak with her about it. If your loved one would like additional support resources, one of the first places to start is asking to speak with a physician.

Ask if you can attend one of her appointments and if she is comfortable with you bringing up your concerns. Alternatively, you can ask her whether she is comfortable with you asking your own family physician about suggested resources in your area.

Work on Self-Care

Try not to neglect your own mental health. The experience of being a new or expecting partner or other integral member of a woman's support network can also be associated with stress, anxiety, or depression. Unfortunately there are limited resources for new partners or other family members. If you are struggling with heightened stress, anxiety, or depression we suggest taking the following steps:

- Speak with your partner about your own sources of stress, anxiety, or depression. We have found that being open about your own concerns can lead to more open and supportive communication for you as well and the sense that you are working on these challenges as a team.

- Speak with your family doctor about counseling or other mental health services. If you have attended a prenatal course, contacting the individual or organization who ran this course may also provide you with information about additional resources.

- Speak with other partners, friends, family members, or members of your support network in the perinatal period. You may find that you are not alone in your concerns.

- Look for online support groups for new fathers, partners, or other family members.

Summing It All Up

Building and maintaining a strong social support network and maximizing the resources that are available to you is essential when raising children, even when a new mother or mother-to-be is not struggling with anxiety or depression. When mental health issues are present, this social support becomes even more critical. In this chapter, we discussed suggestions and strategies to increase this support, including ways of gathering more information, planning ahead for challenging times in the next months, and strategies for reducing barriers to resources. This chapter also included reading intended for loved ones or other members of your support network who may wish to help but be unsure how to proceed.

References

Butler, A. C., Chapman, J. E., Forman, E. M., & Beck, A. T. (2006). The empirical status of cognitive-behavioral therapy: A review of meta-analyses. *Clinical Psychology Reviews, 26,* 17–31. doi:10.1016/j.cpr.2005.07.003

Chambless, D. L., & Ollendick, T. H. (2001). Empirically supported psychological interventions: Controversies and evidence. *Annual Review of Psychology, 52,* 685–716.

Dennis, C. L., & Ross, L. (2006). Women's perceptions of partner support and conflict in the development of postpartum depressive symptoms. *Journal of Advanced Nursing, 56*(6), 588–599. doi:10.1111/j.1365-2648.2006.04059.x

Figueiredo, B., Field, T., Diego, M., Hernandez-Reif, M., Deeds, O., & Ascencio, A. (2008). Partner relationships during the transition to parenthood. *Journal of Reproductive and Infant Psychology, 26*(2), 99–107. doi:10.1080/02646830701873057

Fonseca, A., & Canavarro, M.C. (2017). Women's intentions of informal and formal help-seeking for mental health problems during the perinatal period: The role of perceived encouragement from the partner. *Midwifery, 50,* 78–85. doi:10.1016/j.midw.2017.04.001 Epub 2017 Apr 5.

Goodman, J. H. (2004). Paternal postpartum depression, its relationship to maternal postpartum depression, and implications for family health. *Journal of Advanced Nursing, 45,* 26–35. doi:10.1046/j.1365-2648.2003.02857.x

Green, S. M., Haber, E., Frey, B. N., & McCabe, R. E. (2015). Cognitive-behavioral group treatment for perinatal anxiety: A pilot study. *Archives of Women's Mental Health, 18,* 631–638. doi:10.1007/s00737-015-0498-z

Marchesi, C., Ossola, P., Amerio, A., Daniel, B. D., Tonna, M., & De Panfilis, C. (2016). Clinical management of perinatal anxiety disorders: A systematic review. *Journal of Affective Disorders, 190*, 543–550. doi:10.1016/j.jad.2015.11.004

Matthey, S., Barnett, B., Howie, P., & Kavanagh, D. J. (2003). Diagnosing postpartum depression in mothers and fathers: Whatever happened to anxiety? *Journal of Affective Disorders, 74*, 139–147. doi:10.1016/S0165-0327(02)00012-5

Rowe, H., Holton, S., & Fisher, J. (2013). Postpartum emotional support: A qualitative study of women's and men's anticipated needs and preferred resources. *Australian Journal of Primary Health, 19*, 46–52. doi:10.1071/PY11117

Stephens, S., Ford, E., Paudyal, P., & Smith, H. (2016). Effectiveness of psychological interventions for postnatal depression in primary care: A meta-analysis. *Annals of Family Medicine, 14*, 463–472. doi:10.1370/afm.1967

Index

Locators in *italics* refer to figures though these are not indexed separately from the principal page spans when occurring concurrently with related text.